Public Speaking for Money

Public Speaking for Money

**INSIDER'S SECRETS TO WORKING WITH AGENTS AND
BUREAUS . . . AND GETTING BOOKED SOLID**

Frank Candy

American Speakers Bureau Corporation - Orlando, Florida

www.speakersbureau.com
www.publicspeakingformoney.com
www.frankcandy.com

ISBN: 0996214607
ISBN 13: 9780996214605
Library of Congress Control Number: 2015904921
American Speakers Bureau, Orlando, FL

Public Speaking for Money

Insider's Secrets to Working with Agents and Bureaus . . . and Getting Booked Solid

- Boost your profits
- Get high quality bookings
- Generate Multiple Streams of massive and passive income
- Discover 89 Ideas you can turn into profit

By Frank Candy
Founder and President
American Speakers Bureau Corporation - Orlando, Florida
www.speakersbureau.com
www.publicspeakingformoney.com
www.frankcandy.com

This book is for professional public speakers. From time to time, I use the acronym F.A.M.E. it is for Film, Actors, Models, Entertainment, and it's not limited to just them.

If you are a writer, author, trainer, consultant, entertainer, actor, artist, magician, musician, model, film director, producer, photographer, professional athlete, coach, broadcast journalist, or have a title or label that requires you to market and sell to clients, work with agents, and get booked, then this book is for you!

Also in this book you will learn how to find, engage, and work with agents at speakers' bureaus, talent agencies, and other similar organizations, plus much more.

The ideas, strategies, tips, and suggestions I am offering you come from real experiences working in the offices, boardroom, lecture halls, and auditoriums all over the world. They stem from my work with speakers, trainers, consultants, entertainers, and many professionals as they worked to earn opportunities, like bookings and projects, and when they were ready, they partnered with an agent and became far more successful.

Consequently, this book contains portions of actual case histories.

Confidentiality is essential to our business and our practice. Therefore, all the case descriptions have had the name, and other particulars, altered so as to preserve the anonymity of our clients and friends, without distorting the essential reality of our experiences with each other.

Testimonials

I chased Frank Candy for ten years until I caught him. His industry knowledge is unmatched. He was and is the front-runner in the speaking and consulting industry and has infinite "new" knowledge, as in secrets to generating new business, wowing clients, and navigating the new digital economy.

If you want to achieve great success, study and learn from the master. Beyond his engaging personality, warm smile, and super-friendly demeanor; Frank is brilliant, a genius, and will continue to lead this industry. Get out your highlighter; get out your notepad, "Public Speaking for Money" is filled with treasures; including crucial business intelligence. Frank provides you with a map to unlimited success.

Brian Holloway
Author and Professional Speaker
Three-time NFL Pro Bowler and Super Bowl XX veteran

As a professional speaker for over 40 years, a Professor of Communications for three major universities, and as a professional Coach, I can testify that this book is a touchdown, a home run, and a hole-in-one, all at once between these covers.

There are many books, going back over a hundred years, which will offer you suggestions on how to write and deliver a speech; this book is the ultimate guide to earn paid bookings.

I wish I had this information when I started my professional speaking career in the 1970's. The Chapters on how it works, publishing, and working with agents are priceless.

This book is required reading for anyone who expects to be paid for speaking and hopes to build a career as an author, authority, motivator, or celebrity.

Dr. Johnny Miller, CSP
Author, Keynote Speaker, Seminar Leader, Professor, and
Sportsman

As Senior VP for the NBA's Orlando Magic, the author of over 80 books and a frequent motivational speaker, I always thought I had learned pretty much everything about public speaking. Then along comes this brilliant book from my long-time friend and agent, Frank Candy. I'm a firm believer in Frank and this book! It's truly an encyclopedia about success in the public speaking business.

Pat Williams
Basketball Hall of Fame
Senior VP, NBA's Orlando Magic

This book is an invaluable reference for anybody who wants to share his or her story with the world. Success in any endeavor requires strategy, planning, resource management, desire, and effort.

If you have a deep desire, and are willing to put forth the effort, this book will give you the plans and strategies to make it happen, and will save you a bunch of money and time in the process.

Captain Mike Penn
U.S. Navy Fighter Pilot
POW, Vietnam War
Commercial Airline Pilot, Check Pilot, Chief Pilot, and Flight Manager
Southwest Airlines

Since winning the Olympic Gold Medal in Nagano, Japan, in 1998, I've tapped into Frank Candy's wealth of public speaking and promotional knowledge. Frank's assistance improved my distinguished career as a popular professional speaker for many Fortune 500 companies.

Like any successful athlete, I knew that I needed the right coach to get me to the podium. Many people have given me suggestions over the years, but nothing came close to the wisdom, tactics, and tools, that Frank shared.

If you buy one book to launch or elevate your speaking career, "Public Speaking for Money" is it. It easily wins the gold medal from me. This is the best investment you can make in your speaking career.

Nikki Stone
Olympic Gold Medalist, Professional Speaker, Corporate Performance Seminar Coach, and Amazon Bestselling Author

As a seasoned professional speaker (27 years in the business probably makes me a bit over-seasoned) I truly enjoyed reading Frank Candy's insightful book, "Public Speaking for Money."

It offers everything a new speaker needs to know to get noticed and hired by speakers bureaus. As a professional speaker and owner of a speakers bureau himself, Frank offers tons of tips that are accompanied by engaging personal stories that illustrate not only what the new speaker should do, but why it works.

For example, he tells a story about how the bartender didn't show up for a speaking engagement he was hired to do, so Frank volunteered to tend bar until it was time for him to go on stage. The client loved it and reported back to the bureau how pleased she was that Frank was willing to do what it took to make the engagement successful. Frank has since done several more engagements for that bureau.

I also loved this book because it reminded me of things I should be doing to maintain my relationships with the bureaus with whom I work.

The bottom line here is whether you are a new speaker or a seasoned one; Public Speaking for Money is a worth-while read. I hope you enjoy it as much as I did.

Larry Johnson,
CSP Speaker, author and corporate culture expert, is the coauthor of the highly acclaimed, top-selling book, "Absolute Honesty: Building A Corporate Culture That Values Straight Talk And Rewards Integrity."

If any man on this planet walks the walk and talks the talk, it's Frank Candy. Since 1997, I have hired Frank as a consultant, mentor, and for several marketing and brand development projects for my speaking and entertainment carrier. Dollar for dollar and pound for pound, he is the best there is. He is indeed the true rock star of the speaking and entertainment industry.

The man doesn't sleep and he's like a human computer of knowledge and wisdom based on his research and personal experiences.

With his vast resume of experience and having been on both sides of the public speaking as an agent, speaker bureau owner, and professional speaker, his new book, "Public Speaking For Money" should be a must read for every speaker, trainer, and entertainer who is starting out, or reinventing, or launching into a new market or new product for your public speaking and entertainment career.

Marvelless Mark.
Las Vegas Headliner, International and Award-Winning Entertainer
Corporate Speaker and MC, and
Author: Opportunity Rocks! Be a Rock Star in Business and Beyond

I have known Frank Candy since 1992, and I've hired Frank Candy to deliver over 30 speeches in seven states. I wrote about him in my book "The Obvious Expert" mentioning him in four different places. Each time Frank spoke for my groups, he inspired the audience to overcome the adversity of tough times, build a relevant business that really matters, and inspired them to go to a higher level. I have been asking Frank Candy to write this book for over a decade. You hold in your hands the Bible for making big money as a public speaker.

**Elsom Eldridge. – NGH, New Hampshire
Author of "How To Position Yourself As The Obvious Expert, Turbocharge Your Consulting or Coaching Business Now" (http://obvious-expert.com)
Co-author with Dan Kennedy: "The Ultimate Home Study Action Course for Maximum Success in the Consulting Business"
Co-author with Howard Shenson: "The Consulting Encyclopedia"
Co-creator: "Course for Certified Professional Marketing Consultant" (http://www.cpmc.com)**

I am a big fan of Frank Candy's new book, "Public Speaking for Money." If you really think you can speak to strangers for money, listen to Frank's perspective as a speaker and as a top tier speaker's agent. He's seen it all...and since you haven't yet...take Frank's word as Gold.

Ross Shafer
6-time Emmy Award Winner, Best-selling author of the books: "Are You Relevant?" "The Customer Shouts Back," "Nobody Moved Your Cheese," "Grab more Market Share," and "Absolutely Necessary." Ross Shafer is a CPAE Hall of Fame professional speaker.

Foreword

Astronaut and Space Shuttle Commander Rick Searfoss.

In my former career, I was a fighter pilot and test pilot with the U.S. Air Force, always dreaming of one day becoming an astronaut. So I was ecstatic when NASA selected me to be an astronaut, one of just 7 pilots in a class of 23 out of 2500 applicants. Subsequently I flew three Space Shuttle Missions, as Pilot for STS-58 and 76 and Commander of STS-90 on Columbia.

One of the extra duties of being an astronaut is to give public presentations representing NASA and the Space Program. Unlike many of my colleagues, I found that I thoroughly enjoyed public speaking. From audience feedback, I also discovered that audiences really enjoyed my presentations as well. For example, Dr. Stephen R. Covey, author of The Seven Habits of Highly Effective People, heard one of my speeches given when I was still in the Astronaut Corps. We met afterwards, and he personally counseled me that the business world could benefit from my decades of leadership and team experiences coupled with the inspirational way I customize my presentations for each audience.

Thus was born the idea of becoming a professional "Astronaut Speaker." I was confident I had superb real-world content, experiences, and stories. I was comfortable on stage. But how was I to make the transition from speaking to NASA audiences as a side duty to giving relevant, value-added professional presentations for business audiences?

Fortunately, I connected with Frank Candy at the American Speakers Bureau early in that transition. What started as a discussion over pancakes at breakfast one beautiful Florida morning, blossomed into a great friendship and long-term business relationship.

Right from the start Frank was very giving with his tips, recommendations, and suggestions for getting ahead in the world of professional speaking. He radically increased my learning curve! All of those strategies and much more are in this book, <u>Public Speaking for Money</u>.

Frank kept working with me to fine tune my brand, marketing, and positioning as a high-content expert, celebrity, author, thought-leader and astronaut who speaks.

Looking back, I see many similarities between flying a rocket ship into space and achieving success as a professional speaker.

First, the need for "no-stone-unturned" preparation and rehearsal is just as important launching a speaking career, as the thousands of hours of real flying time and practicing in flight simulators prior to a human space launch. This book includes the keys to accelerating that preparation: how to overcome issues, obstacles, and adversities quickly, and make the most of every opportunity.

Next, a Space Shuttle Commander must focus on every aspect of the overall mission. Absolutely nothing can be neglected. A speaker must likewise build every element of their career, on and off the stage. Marketing, promotion, branding all matter; as well as, of course, an exquisite performance on the platform.

Third, although the astronauts and the speakers get the glory when things go well, behind each space mission and each event there is a team of great people working very diligently in the background. These are the flight managers, engineers, agents, and meeting and event planners that are working behind the spotlight rather than in it. They too are striving for excellence and mastery. A truly successful astronaut or speaker must constantly think "team," and reinforce and build up those who support their work.

Fourth, in the Air Force and NASA, self-promoting is not encouraged. We let our actions and flying speak for us. In public speaking, of course, it is a necessary and important aspect; though for me it was a difficult transition. Personally, I finally broke the secret code thanks to Frank's tips and counsel that "if you truly believe that you have an inspirational message that matters, you'll overcome your reservations about telling the world that belief!" You'll find similar superb ideas in this book to assist you as you constantly promote and update your marketing and branding.

So, do you think you have the courage to head out onto the stage and the launch pad? If so, be willing to prepare like your life depends on it, work to learn and execute on every aspect of the speaking business, build extensive relationships with your mission support team, and believe in yourself enough to effectively market and sell your services to a world that needs what you have to offer. If you apply its lessons, this book can be your Mission Control in every one of those areas!

Building and maintaining a successful public speaking career, like flying Space Shuttles, requires hard work, dedication, and focus; it is not for the timid or bashful. If you follow Frank's recommendations, suggestions, tips, ideas, and advice, you will cut your learning time dramatically. So strap in, start the countdown, and launch yourself off the pad! It's time for you to rocket past the rest of the pack!

Rick Searfoss, Colonel, U.S. Air Force Retired

Astronaut/Space Shuttle Commander

The "Astronaut Speaker" and the only astronaut in history to earn the Certified Speaking Professional designation from the National Speakers Association

Introduction

This book is about the future, and about YOU and how you can be a public speaker for money in the future!

In the 1950's and 60's my mother was selling real estate, so as a child I was attending big sales rallies with her. At those rallies, I saw, met, and experienced many of the great speakers of the day.

Some of them included:

- Dr. Norman Vincent Peale, public speaker, minister, and author of *The Power of Positive Thinking*
- Art Linkletter, CPAE, Radio and TV personality
- Og Mandino, Class of 1980, inducted into Speakers Hall of Fame, went on to sell over 35 million books
- Jim Rohn, CPAE, received numerous industry awards in the speaking industry. Jim's philosophies and influence continue to have worldwide impact.
- Earl Nightingale, personal development pioneer and radio legend
- Judge Ziglar, the older brother of Zig Ziglar and author of *Timid Salesmen have Skinny Kids*
- *Zig Ziglar who was such an inspiration to so many and a great speaker to work with*
- Ken McFarland, Dean of American Public Speakers

- Cavett Robert, Class of 1972, Founder of The National Speakers Association Inducted into Speakers Hall of Fame. Namesake of the coveted Cavett Award
- Bill Gove, Bill Gove, CSP, CPAE, was recognized around the world as the father of professional speaking. Toastmasters International awarded Bill Gove its Golden Gavel Award in 1991, and called him one of the most popular speakers of the 20th Century
- Ira Hayes, CPAE, author of *Yak, Yak, Yak* and *Success, Go For It*. He delivered more than 4,000 presentations around the world
- Brian Townsend, CSP, CPAE, who was a great friend, business partner, and one of the early inspirations to write this book. 10% of the proceeds from this book will be going to charities Brian and I agreed on.

And so many more, however, this book is about the future, not the past. Maybe down the road, I will write one about the past, but for now this book is about you and what you can do make money as a public speaking and entertainer for money in the future!

For over 40 years I have been booking, promoting, and organizing lectures, concerts, and conventions, sometimes all in one day! As I look back, some of it was like living a great dream. Not all of it, but most of it. This is my story.

In the early '70's, I started out as a participatory photo-journalist, entertainment booker, and show promoter. I was backstage with great speakers and music groups from Motown and Rock, like The Temptations, The Spinners, Fleetwood Mac, America, Eagles, Joe Walsh, and many more. One memorable night in John Belushi's dressing room we hung out with Hunter Thompson; then another night we were backstage with Jimmy Buffet, helping big security guys hold the door shut to keep the groupies and other question-able characters out.

In the late 1970's, I changed career paths more than a couple times, and there was a moment when I realized I could use this platform to create good by influencing people with my story, energy, strategies and leadership. Eventually I became a full-time public speaker, author, promoter for lectures and training, and an agent. Consciously I made the switch hoping I would live longer, so far so good.

It's been a long strange trip and along the way, I chose this path with no regrets. I believe I have lived a very blessed and exciting life by looking for the American Dream, learning to be grateful and believe in myself.

Gratitude is a powerful process for shifting your energy and bringing more of what you want into your life. Be grateful for what you already have and you will attract more good things. It's a good philosophy to live by.

Now, I am at the part of life that is labeled as pre-retirement, and considering changing paths again; it's like a re-wiring of my life, where I am looking back, and looking ahead; the good news is, I still have good health (well, I woke up and had a pulse!) and I have hope! Lots and lots of hope!

THE ONE THING
ALL FAMOUS AUTHORS,
WORLD CLASS ATHLETES,
BUSINESS TYCOONS,
SINGERS, ACTORS, AND
CELEBRATED ACHIEVERS
IN ANY FIELD
HAVE IN COMMON IS THIS,
THEY BEGAN THEIR JOURNEYS
WHEN THEY WERE
NONE OF THESE THINGS.

Contents

■ communicate with the agents promptly ■ Meeting professionals want to feel your commitment to their meeting's success

■ A way of looking at things ■ A way of life ■ Mediocrity is such an unfulfilling form of existence - Mastery is an extremely pleasing feeling when one finally gets on top of a new set of skills, and then sees the light through the new door those skills can open for them ■ Master/Expert. Masters and experts create new knowledge ■ You will be a better person ■ a better friend ■ a better boyfriend/girlfriend ■ husband/wife ■ and employee ■ You will be a better everything ■ This is your show, your future, and your life ■ I only offer advice and strategy, the answer lies within you

■ Anticipate problems and issues - Be a part of the team. Walk a mile in their shoes, be humble, be willing to do what-ever-it-takes to make the entire show a success, and play to win ■ You should always be kind. Everyone you meet is fighting a battle you know nothing about ■ You will be judged by your last speech, your last performance, and your last assignment ■ Make sure it is the best you can do every single time

              ▪ An Overview of the history of the Economy ▪ The
              Political Influences – How the events of 9-11 changed
              our world and industry forever - The popular speak-
              ers with great branding ▪ relevant information like
              competitive market intelligence, get booked often
              ▪ The four common denominators remained constant:
              Branding, marketing, good platform skills, and repu-
              tation they matter ▪ Audiences want in-depth learn-
              ing from people who have been there and done it
              ▪ Even the established speaker, will need to re-pack-
              age their background and topics with a strong brand,
              for the ever-changing, multi-cultural, multi-tasking,
              multi-generational workforce ▪ thousands of speakers
              are booked every day for money and you need to ask
              the right questions like: How did they do it? And WHY
              were they chosen?

              ▪ Sponsorship enables you to proactively reach the
              right people and create results that matter, and pro-
              vide more exposure and more options than you ever
              thought possible ▪ What if you could book 10, or 25,
              or 50 events with one client over the next three of
              four months? ▪ Imagine going on a speaking tour of
              the country, or the world, and going first-class, staying
              in fine hotels, eating great food, meeting wonderful
              people who adore you, and autographing thousands
              of books along the way. ▪ **Are you living the dream?**
              ▪ **If not then invest in this book.** ▪ The "ROI" factors
              - ROI can stand for Return on Investment ▪ Return on

involvement ▪ or Return on Innovation ▪ Sponsorship is a popular and growing opportunity for the right situation. ▪ You need to know the game and the rules before jumping in.

The world of grants is complicated and not for the faint of heart ▪ Here is what you need to know ▪ Primarily grants come from private foundations, companies, and government agencies. The majority of the time the grants are awarded to non-profit groups. Where do you start ▪ there is an art and science to it ▪ There is a process, and procedure, rules and regulations, it has its own set of terms and is very technical. Don't be scared off ▪ You will know if it's for you because the answer lies within you.

▪ Earning Bookings With Governments in the USA and Around the World ▪ Booking work with the government is doable and fun ▪ However it is not easy and usually complicated ▪ Each department, bureau, division ▪ and group and is different ▪ focus on exactly what they want and need ▪ and how to deliver it ▪ and how to get paid ▪ Make friends with at least one person within the government ▪ who knows how things work ▪ and how to get things done ▪ every "t" must be crossed ▪ every "I" must be dotted ▪ follow the steps and process of filings ▪ hearings ▪ interviews ▪ approvals ▪ Every government agency ▪ department ▪ group and entity has its own codes ▪ acronyms and language ▪ The more you learn and know, the better and faster you will become with the process ▪ Get ready for acronym hell ▪ CCR ▪ POC ▪ EB POC ▪ D&B DUNS ▪ IRS ▪ TIN ▪ EIN ▪ SAM ▪ CCR ▪ POC ▪ EB POC ▪ D&B ▪ DUNS ▪ IRS ▪ TIN ▪ EIN ▪ SAM ▪ Cage Code ▪ CAGE Verification ▪ SBA and more.

CHAPTER 1

The Magical Mystery Tour
Understand the Market and the Business

"Seek First to Understand, Then to Be Understood."
Steven R. Covey, The Seven Habits of Highly Effective People.

Think about the really big picture. Here is the insider's secret. How much is a speakers bureau worth to you? If you do it right, it could be worth millions of dollars. On the average, most of the agencies and bureaus have several thousand clients in their database. For a solo speaker, trainer, corporate entertainer, or consultant, that could be a lifetime of work.

Now, let's assume you played the game right, (by the plans I describe and reveal in this book), and you earn a place on the roster of 20 or more speakers bureaus, and they have (on average) 5,000 clients in their database. That's 100,000 potential opportunities for bookings, if you are really good.

Now, if you work the plan right, and you establish a good reputation and track record with bureaus, and work with just say 10 or 20 of them, and they each book for an average of 10 events a year, hey - do the numbers. It's like outsourcing your marketing department, and the cost is much less. Cha-ching! (That is urban slang for a big cash register.)

Just look at the speakers who are booked regularly by the agents at a speakers bureau.

A former national football coach, or an author with some name recognition, earns 30K to 60K (or more) per speech, and gets booked just 100 times a year. That's three to six million bucks for a job that requires no heavy lifting, no late nights, and he can pick and choose the clients, cities, and events he wants to do. Now, add the perks of first-class travel, nice resort hotels and suites, book sales, personal appearances and product endorsements, and you can double or tipple the income. Cha-ching!

If winning isn't everything, why do they keep score? - Vince Lombardi

If you don't have celebrity or icon status, but you have a popular book, or multiple books out there, then cut that down conservatively to one-third, and your net profit after commissions could be 750K to over a million. You wouldn't be reading menus from right to left if you were making six or seven figures a year.

The moment of truth: This does not work for everyone. You can't put a square peg in a round hole.

Now let's get realistic: If you developed (or plan on developing) a strong and recognizable brand, created and wrote a popular book, or books, executed a powerful and well-designed marketing plan, established yourself as a recognized expert in your field, created reasons for thousands of people to like you, became popular in social media, have a proven track record of delivering a likable speech in a marketplace that is known to pay thousands of dollars for speakers, and booked a couple hundred speeches in the marketplace, then you are in the minority. Matter of fact, you are the professional speaker that the leaders and agents at the agencies and bureaus would like to add to their roster.

Your life is in your hands. No matter where you are now, no matter what has happened in your life, you can begin to consciously choose your thoughts, and you can change your life. There is no such thing as a hopeless situation. Every single circumstance of your life can change. **From the book: The Secret.**

Sidebar for a moment: It's hard to find people who agree on just when the first speakers bureau was established.

The truth is, it is only somewhat relevant to this book, so this treatise will end quickly.

Perhaps they started in Ancient Greece, and one of the great speakers was Demosthenes. He delivered his speech, "On the Crown", in Athens in 330 B.C., urging loyalty and honesty in politics. (What a concept!) It is still considered a model of speechmaking. I am only bringing it up because it is still a good message for today, and those are good core principles of this business. And I expect someone probably arranged for Demosthenes to show up that day, and handled some of the details.

The young people I had lunch with today thought I was there in Ancient Greece, plus served in the American Revolution too. For a moment I wanted to dope slap them so hard even Google couldn't find them, but then I realized to them I am old, and I am getting too crabby!

Thank you for indulging me; now let us start to unlock the secrets of the Magical Mystery Tour.

Are you a new speaker, trainer, musician, artist, athlete, or actor? Then this is a great place to start! Are you are an established speaker or artist of any type? Then this book is filled with suggestions, tips, and wisdom, plus new profit centers, and will be a good reference book for you.

Just so you don't get discouraged; I have assisted many good people in going up to the next level in this business, and launched the careers of some truly great people. I am going to reveal how I did it for them, and how you can do it too in today's ever changing, multi-generational, multi-cultural, multi-ethnic, high-tech, high-risk, and international workplace we find ourselves in.

CHAPTER 2

Several Ways To Get Paid As A Public Speaker

The most common way is to get booked for an event by a company or group, and earn a speaking fee.

The second way is to speak for free in return for exposure. I have rarely been in favor of that model. Some people have died from exposure, and others have been arrested for it! (I hope you are laughing!)

There are exceptions, just like the secrets, and each situation needs to be evaluated for its merits.

One of the key factors to consider if you agree to do a free event in an industry you are known in and popular: You run the risk of reducing your value. On the other hand if you want to penetrate the industry, then it might work. The secret is to look at the big picture, and know your long-term outcome.

Some of the things you could negotiate include: (This secret is worth thousands of dollars.) Asking them to record your program in high-definition digital video. You would receive a copy of the master, and you could offer to sell them the rights to use your presentation for in-house training, marketing future events, and membership recruitment. Be sure to put it in writing, and include the terms for making copies, distribution, sales, and marketing if they plan to sell them, you might ask for a percentage of the profit.

They could agree to let you sell your products, and you could ask for the contact list of the attendees.

It never hurts to ask. I recommend you have these ideas and offers ready to discuss when the opportunity is on the table, and not after you signed the contract.

There are situations that warrant doing things pro-bono. There is value in selling an idea to supporters, asking investors for funding on a project, or as I did a few years ago, inspiring a city council to move in favor of an important issue in our community.

The free model may be interpreted or understood as part of your job description. Law enforcement agencies, schools, hospitals, utility, power, and cable companies, and many more groups like these have small speakers bureaus often run by the public relations department where representatives will go out in the community to discuss many topics that fall within their jurisdiction and expertise. In most cases the speaker is an employee of the school, agency, utility or company, and receives a paycheck for their job, so in essence, they are getting paid to talk.

Then there is the old model of selling a product. This one is high risk and high reward. The business model of making money by selling products goes back longer than I have been on the planet. (Please don't be like my close friends' grandkids and ask if I fought in the Civil War!)

Over the years I have watched professional speakers and pitchmen and women deliver a very tightly choreographed presentation from about one to two hours, and the best ones sell over six figures worth of product in the back of the room, or the auditorium hallways. Note: Some events may have several thousand people in attendance.

Zig Ziglar was a master at doing this. He told me if the conditions are right, and there have been no outside distractions or dramas in the news that day, and the room temperature was right, and PA system worked well, and the people working the product tables were efficient and fast, and the sun, the moon and the stars all lined up just right, and he was blessed that day by the Lord, he would do very well.

Doing a stand-up presentation for the purpose of selling products or services to 50, or 500, or 5,000 or 50,000, is a very different presentation with complex dynamics, compared to the typical keynote speech to a group of corporate executives, teachers, or trades people.

If your purpose is to sell your products or services, then you better be very good and effective real fast, or you will starve.

The first time I did this kind of presentation, I fell short of my expectation for the sales. Nevertheless I exceeded the event promoter's expectations by over 16%.

The reason, I believed I missed the mark, and did not meet my potential was because as I was reading the audience, it was my belief I did not engage them deeply enough. I felt I missed making a strong case for some key points and did not deliver a compelling argument, or a convincing close to the sale, and so I could have inspired more of them to get out a credit card, checkbook, or cash, and give us the money.

So there you go, several models: Free for exposure, or a purpose, the get paid by your job to make a presentation, or hired by a group or booked by an agent, or booked by a promoter to sell your products and you earn a share of the profit. The more you sell, the more you make.

The last one is worthy of some more specifics.

One of the ways to do this is what I call delivering the presentation with the pain and gain method.

The speaker opens up with a story to connect with them on as many levels as possible. This speaker can get them involved and take them for a fun journey that looks, sounds, smells, and feels like a near life disaster that becomes a miracle as they invite them for a roller coaster ride, like an epic adventure, with excitement and danger that involves near death experiences, winning the big lottery a couple times, and finding the fountain of youth.

The products they are selling claim to make them younger, healthier, happier, sexier, smarter and richer than anyone can imagine.

And if they make the bad choice to not buy it today at the vastly reduced discount price, they will surely suffer, or worse, die an agonizing death.

So for only 1,997 dollars...no wait they say, "I like you because you are like me, shrewd, smart, and sophisticated..."

They continue, "So I am going to give you my special friends and family discount for half price. But wait there's more! Our sponsor or promoter made me sweeten the deal of a lifetime by including a two-for-one package, a discount to my latest seminar, and the too good to be true, audio recordings and workbooks for solving all of life's mysteries, fixing the government, curing all sickness and poverty, saving the whales and the puppies, solving homelessness and hunger, and even fixing Congress."

They take a long pause and say, "Just hurry and get out your credit card and run to the table in the back of the room because we brought a limited supply, and the darn shipping company lost one of the crates, so we don't have enough for everybody."

Some of the best people I have witnessed doing this use hypnosis and subliminal messages to persuade people to buy their stuff.

Sorry, I took off on a rant. But just for once I wish someone will stand up there and just tell us the damn truth!

The majority of speakers' bureaus have not included this "sell-product and earn a percentage of the commission" option in their business model, in part because it is difficult to measure, control and even understand. It's like the consumer price index. I have yet to experience two politicians explain it the same way.

Now over the years I have booked speakers for large groups with no honorarium or fee, and no commission, and no allowance for expenses. The only profit option was a percentage for product sales. When I took the risk, most of the time I was rewarded very well with commissions from product sales.

One of my friends, who has been a very successful agent for many years, has completely avoided those kinds of situations and clients. He said simply, "It is not a flavor I enjoy." That's his choice.

Over time, I've had it come to light later that some of the prominent speakers we booked earned spin-off business and more bookings, and much more product sales after the event – for which we were paid nothing. We don't book those people anymore.

In summary:

There are many business models that could work for you. Each opportunity has its pros and cons. Be sure to do your research, understand the secrets and combinations, take care of your agent, and leave no stone unturned.

CHAPTER 3

How the Game Works – Unlocking The Secrets
The Big Picture and Big Money
Walk a Mile in My Shoes

Being a paid, professional public speaker is one of the few lucrative markets that do not require a college degree or certification, and you don't need protective gear!

You don't have to be skinny, good looking, sing in tune or play music! But you do have to accomplish something relevant to talk about, so people are inspired to listen to you.

The fact is, some popular and well-paid speakers are ex-convicts who paid their debt to society and decided to work in this profession.

Moment of truth: You need to know how the speaking business works, you need to understand the professional speaking and entertainment industry, and you need to know the rules, terms, procedures, and policies for the business. Furthermore, you need to know how to market yourself and develop partnerships with people who can move you forward.

Many of the jobs that will exist ten and twenty years from now do not exist yet. Except for public speaking, training, entertaining and consulting. They will still be in demand.

Rule Number 1, Get Real!

Before you decide to call an agent at a speakers bureau, be sure you are 100% ready to make that move. The people I have consulted with over the years have all been told the same thing, and in virtually every case it was true.

Have your media kit in hard copy with a DVD of your demo reel(s), have this also on YouTube, autographed copies of your books, all bureau friendly one sheets, and a agent friendly website ready and battle tested.

Moment of Truth: Hire a real consultant with experience in this business to make sure your media kit works. There are plenty of them like me out there. The time and money you invest to work with them will be well worth it.

Word of caution, I have watched many speakers, authors, and entertainers hire advertising agencies to develop their press kits and demos. The majority of the time they failed to deliver the best results. I have nothing against advertising agencies or the people who work in them. The good ones are worth their weight in gold, but finding the right people to do the right job can be like doing your own root canal.

Here is a good place to start:

When you interview someone, ask him or her, these eight questions:

What are you going to do for me?

Have you completed projects like this one you are proposing to produce and complete for me?

Will you show me what you did for them?

Will you offer a list of names and numbers for references?

How well do you know the market?

How long will it take?

How much will it cost?

What do you guarantee for results?

If you like the answers, you believe they are being honest with you, and you trust them, then hire them, if not, move on to the next one. Lastly, I would require a face-to-face meeting with them to ask them these questions. Making a big decision like this over the phone is not a good practice.

This is a relationship-driven business that starts with earning and building real trust, with most, if not all of the people at the bureau. Years ago when I moved the company from Ohio to Florida, I hired an office manager named Pamela. She became a wonderful and trusted friend. She retired, and we are still friends. Pamela helped us screen speakers and trainers - and Lord forbid a speaker would be rude or treat her poorly. Not treating her or anyone else at the company with respect was a guaranteed way for your media kit to hit the circular file and get your name on the "Do Not Book" list.

On average, we received 150 requests per week from speakers, authors, coaches, athletes, experts, retiring executives, and retiring military personnel. It is overwhelming. And it's only going to get worse as the Baby-Boomers retire because they want to keep earning money.

So how do you set yourself apart from the herd?

Your opinion of how good you are is not relevant. Matter of fact, a well-known and very respected agent who has been in the business longer than me said: "In all the years I have been in the business, never once has a new speaker called me and said, 'I am just an average speaker. Almost every time they launch into a one-sided discussion about how great they are.'"

Don't do that! It's simply not a good way to start a relationship that requires honesty, good communication, and mutual respect. Your relationship with this agent could be worth a many thousands or a couple million dollars, or much more to you. Do it right the first time.

There is no agent or speaker bureau that will book you because you think you are good. They will not even book you because *they* think you are good. Get real!

As with most goods and services in a free market, the one true judge of quality and value is the market. Agents only recommend and book, and event planners only hire, the speakers and trainers who have earned respect and demand (popularity) from the marketplace.

While this is frustrating at the beginning of a speaking career, this is the way it is. This is the market's way of flushing out the unqualified, the unwilling, and the undeserving.

You just have to be willing to market yourself and sell yourself until you have established credibility in the market. You have to prove to the agents the marketing you created for you works.

Many musicians who made it big started out in small clubs and even on street corners. Athletes who make it to the pros had to pay their dues in high school, college and the minor leagues.

The same is true with speakers, trainers, and FAME.

The same is true with most professions. There is one exception, and that was the mortgage industry in 2003 – 2007. Our favorite waiter at the bagel shop and our pizza delivery guy both became mortgage brokers, and you know what happened there.

Secondly, you will not appreciate the effort, work, risk, and massive undertaking of the agents and speakers' bureau role in your career until you have done it yourself.

Reminds me of the lyrics to a good song…

"Walk A Mile In My Shoes" By Joe South and made famous by Elvis Presley

If I could be you, if you could be me, for just one hour
If we could find a way to get inside each other's mind
If you could see you through my eyes instead of your ego
I believe you'd be, surprised to see
That you've been blind
Walk a mile in my shoes
Walk a mile in my shoes
Yeah, before you abuse, criticize and accuse
Walk a mile in my shoes

Now there are people on reservations
And out in the ghetto
And brother there, but for the grace of God go you and I
If I only had the wings of a little angel
Don't you know, I'd fly to the top of a mountain
And then I'd cry, cry, cry
Walk a mile in my shoes
Walk a mile in my shoes
Yeah, before you abuse, criticize and accuse walk a mile in my shoes

Get Real: Do not expect the agent of the bureau to make you an immediate success.

You need to create your own niche in the market; you and only you are responsible for your success.

Even if an agent at a bureau agrees to promote you and put you on their roster, it will take some time to get your name, brand and topic out to the market. There is a timing factor that is the nature of the market too.

Most big meetings are planned six months, a year, or even two years or more in advance.

While the trend over the last twenty years is for a shorter time-line to secure the speaker for the next meeting or round of meetings, a majority of events are set well enough in advance that it will take time getting your name into the cycle of awareness and consideration by committees for future events.

Every business, every entrepreneur, and professional public speaker, trainer, musician and entertainer will have to constantly work on three things.

1. Innovation and creativity. For speakers: writing and rehearsing speeches, creating products like books and training programs; plus, inventing marketing plans, websites, and maintaining social media.
2. Execution. The implementation of number one, printing out uncorrected galley proofs of your book to test in the market, sending it out for evaluation, testimonials, and beta testing, eventually publishing your books and products, rolling out your marketing plan for testing and trying out your material like George Carlin would do at hundreds of live performances in comedy clubs around the country before he would perfect the show and make it one of his legendary 14 HBO Comedy Specials. George told me he put well over a thousand hours into writing, rehearsing, and perfecting each one-hour show for HBO. How much are you willing to put in?

On May 3, 1975, Glen Frey (Co-founder of the Eagles, with Don Henley) told me the Eagles would practice a song one hundred times in a row perfectly, before, they ever played it live in concert. If you were lucky enough to attend an Eagles' concert, then you know how amazing and tight their performances were.

Late in his career, best-selling author and very popular motivational speaker Zig Ziglar told me he would still practice and rehearse at least three hours for every hour he was going to be onstage before a show. And at that time he had been on stage over 30 years!

Too many times speakers, trainers, comedians, actors, and entertainers told me after a sub-par performance; they were rusty, or out of practice, or they did not connect with the audience, or the lights were too bright, or the stage was too high or too low, or the shape of the room was odd, or the acoustics sucked, or the size of teleprompter was wrong, or there was a short microphone wire, or their pants were to tight ... so many more excuses.

It was clear to me in virtually every case that they failed to research the audience, pay attention to the details, or put in the time to show up for a walk through, sound checks, and rehearse in advance.

One time, I watched a professional speaker deliver a very robust and entertaining performance in Daytona Beach for a business group. She was very good and delivered a strong and impressive program.

After her program, she revealed to me she had a migraine headache. I would have never known because she did a very good presentation.

She was not the only one. I watched comedian Elayne Boosler deliver an excellent show in Las Vegas for one of our clients, and she had a debilitating migraine. The show must go on, and it should be the very best it can humanly be, every time.

The one excuse that really gets me is: "They booked it late, and I only had three weeks to prepare." Hey, try being a player on a championship team and tell your coach you are not ready. You will be sitting on the bench for the big game, and replaced by a player who is ready.

For the up and coming professional speaker, they need to be practicing long before they get booked for speeches, and I recommend recording them for replay and technique analysis so they can tweak and improve the timing, phraseology, tone, volume, and choreography. You could, and probably should, hire speech coaches to help you tune up your show.

It is advisable for you to hire a performance coach. I have hired several in the past, and each one made me a better speaker and performer.

3. Measure, quantify, and calculate your results. If your marketing plan calls for making 100 calls per day, then you should measure how many real people you spoke with that have the power to hire you, not how many receptionists or secretaries you spoke with, or how many voicemails you left for return calls that never happened. Making a hundred calls a day to people who do not have the power to hire speakers or trainers is a waste of time, money, and resources. For the record, that is not an effective way to market you. There are many better ways. Watch for that book coming out next!

You must measure your marketing efforts against your number of paid bookings to determine what is working.

When you give a speech, you should create a scorecard that will assist in measuring what you did, so you can improve it.

You should have a scorecard for building your relationships with agents at bureaus too.

When you call a bureau, and talk to the agent assigned to you (or the owner) in an attempt to secure an agent, you should have a good agenda to inform them about new and improved strategies and tools to book you. Otherwise, you are wasting their time and your time.

Do you have a new book they can use to promote you? How about a new demo reel? How about a new promotional video? Did you just get a national press release? Are you going to be on a round of TV talk shows discussing a trend on a subject you speak about? You better show up with something relevant.

A speaker called last year to tell us he just published another book. It's a cookbook for Vegans. But all of their other books and topics that we book him for are about teamwork and personal development.

Get real: Time is valuable, and time is money. Don't waste it. Make sure what you do is relevant and has real purpose. If you call them and ask, "What have you done for me lately?", they have the right to ask you the same thing.

The moment of truth: Many of the dates booked by most professional speakers come as the result of someone having heard them speak.

How, then, can you accurately evaluate and quantify your work? Put simply, by keeping track of the number of paid spin-off bookings and repeat engagements that result from your presentations.

Every speaker even established speakers should monitor their frequency rate of spin-offs and repeats.

Keeping track of these things is very important and all speakers, trainers, authors, consultants, and entertainers should be vigilant about trying to improve the numbers.

Now there is a no magical formula that says when you book a speech for a group like a Chamber of Commerce, a big software company or a trade association that you should expect seven spin-off speaking dates, four training dates, three consulting projects, and one invitation to join a board of directors.

You get what you get based on how good you were; who was in the audience, how they reacted to you, and what demand in the market exists for you. Your topic and your service earn more business based on that moment in time. You can consult the I Ching or consult an Astrologer for the position of the sun and the moon, or it is like trying to pick a winner at a horse race, it depends on the speed and desire of the horse and the jockey who drives the horse. Your guess is a long shot at best.

Last year one of my speaker friends booked thirty dates (yes 30) off one speech. That was worth about 300 grand. It's like winning the lottery. Nice when it happens.

I know of speakers who say they never get spin-off dates. The sad truth is that most of them only last a couple of years in the business and then flame out.

Moment of truth: Most of the time, meeting and event planners do not recommend or book speakers that they have not heard.

In today's market, it is mandatory that you have a good quality video recording of you delivering a **live speech to an audience**. To ask an agent to consider booking you without a demo video or "sizzle reel" is like a car dealer asking you to buy an expensive car without allowing you to see it or drive it.

In the past, I have arranged for a meeting planner or committee member to attend a live event where a speaker was delivering a presentation. In one case, I had a meeting planner from Colorado fly all the way to Southern California to watch me deliver a presentation. (This was after watching my video!) It became a double win for us because we had booked three of the four speakers who were on stage that afternoon and this person booked me for their next event, and then they booked one of our other speakers for an event in the future. It's nice when things work out.

When I started in this business, meeting planners were willing to take the advice of an agent and book a speaker the agent recommended. In the 60's and 70's, if speakers had their demo reels, they were on film. In the late 1970's, VHS tape became the new normal, and I remember speakers transferring over their films to video. Some of them were so old they were in Black and White! The late, great Ira Hayes, one of the founding members of the National Speakers Association sent us his video and it was really good –and it was in black and white. The video had a certain Frank Capra feel to it!

Special note: It was an honor and privilege to know Ira Hays, CPAE, for many years. He was a great friend and a terrific speaker. Our bureau was booking him regularly until he became ill and passed away.

So I am channeling my friend Ira here. He said, "Be really good, look for ways to get better, always do your best, and play fair."

In today's electronic age, meeting and event planners do not have to see you live and in person. It can be via a DVD or a video file streaming on the Internet, but it does have to happen. There are exceptions to this rule, but it is hard to sustain a professional career without the best marketing tools to make it happen.

You may get many standing ovations. People may wait in line to speak with you after every presentation, and some may say that you are the best speaker they have ever heard! You may even have stacks and stacks of testimonial letters from clients. These things are nice. <u>But a good video that represents what you do is worth its weight in gold</u>.

It doesn't cost anyone any money to give you an ovation, a compliment, or to write you a nice letter. When a meeting planner or event promoter decides to book you, in most cases they are risking their professional reputation, their job, the event's reputation, their livelihood, and their ability to feed their family.

If it is the company owner who's booking you, they will have to get their checkbook out and send some of their hard earned money to you. They have to trust that you will do a good job for them at their function and that you will treat them fairly on expenses.

Repeats & Spin-Off Bookings Are the True Measure of YOUR Performance.

How many times have you been re-booked by the same client? How often do people hire you because they heard you speak somewhere? In the business we call them repeat and spin-off bookings.

If you are not producing repeats and spin-offs frequently, you may need to focus on your material and your presentation before you seek to work with bureaus.

In my humble opinion, this is the least-followed advice in the professional speaking business. Do not make contact with the bureaus before you are ready.

In Summary: You have to be good, you have to be popular, and you have to get real!

Learn how the business works. Invest in yourself. Be willing to pay your dues. Walk a mile in other people's shoes.

Good innovation and creativity will set you apart from the rest of the competition, as long as you test and measure it properly in the market you expect to be successful in.

You need a good demo reel of you live on stage. It needs to be short and to the point.

CHAPTER 4

Networking, Socializing, and Schmoozing Will Not Get You In The Door With an Agent or Bureau.

Professional organizations for speakers, trainers, and consultants are worthy of your consideration. For over 20 years, I was a member of The National Speakers Association and attended the Annual Conventions and Workshops. I belonged to many other professional organizations too.

Now, I have to say these are really nice people and some of them have been friends for over four decades. I could easily fill a chapter (or two or three) with stories about their generosity, brilliance and kindness. A couple of those wonderful people assitrd me in writing and editing this book! But I am saving all that for a different book, this book is for you!

At the conventions for ASTD (American Society for Training and Development) and the National Speakers Association Annual Conventions or workshops, I chose to remove my name badge because so many newcomers in the industry did not know the protocol, game, rules, procedures, or etiquette (perhaps this is just an observation on my part) or they were afflicted with contagious enthusiasm.

Sometimes I would be in an elevator or at a meal function, or worse, a restroom, and they would launch into their speeches in an effort to impress me with their amazing oratory skills. I was not alone, many of my friends in the speakers' bureau industry like Dottie Walters CPAE, Andrea Gold, Nancy Lauterbach, and many more have shared stories of overzealous people hoping to impress a booking agent.

So how do bureaus find and investigate speakers?

Agents and the people who work at bureaus, find out from the market. We ask meeting and event planners, "Who did the keynote at your event last year?"

Then we follow-up with, "How did they do for you?" We discover how they performed on stage, and how they were to work with offstage. This is a very important piece of the puzzle. If the speaker was great on stage, but had a problem with professionalism offstage, oops – big red flag.

All right one quick story. This one is pretty funny, and it has a happy ending.

About 12 years ago I was hired through a bureau on the West Coast to deliver a dinner speech a small group of about 80 high-level executives, and spouses at a very fancy resort near Orlando. The topic was "Connecting with the Customer through Exceptional Customer Service". (I am not going to reveal too many details because I don't want to get anyone in trouble!)

I was the first one from the group to arrive, and the room was already set up. A few of the waiters were putting the finishing touches on the room. I took a moment to connect with them and thank them for making it look so nice. They were very appreciative, and it was apparent their bosses did not believe in compliments or positive reinforcement. (That's in a different book!)

Well, I set up my equipment, went through my checklist with lights, sound, emergency exits, back-up systems, bottles of water, and props. The bartender, Bob, came in and introduced himself, and offered me a drink. I said: "No thanks, I'll pass." I never drink with clients.

The next person to arrive was Mary, the Meeting Planner. We had spoken by phone several times to plan the event, and discussed the details for timing, content, flow, length, the best kind of humor, audience demographics, handouts, and other typical details.

It was nice to meet her in person, make that connection, and have the opportunity to put a face with the voice. Like many meeting planners before an event she was very stressed out and I put her at ease by telling her a funny story. She calmed down a bit with some laughter.

We were close to opening the doors since many of the folks were waiting in the hall when the bartender took off his jacket and told us he was stepping outside for a smoke. Mary, the meeting planner said, "Good idea, I think I'll join you."

Well, Mary came back a couple minutes later and did a quick run through of her checklist and announced to the wait staff that she was about to open the doors.

Then she said: "Where is Bob the bartender?"

Well, as it turns out, according to an employee who saw him outside, Bob was talking with an attractive woman with long blonde hair – and she may have lured him to the parking lot! I am unsure of the rest of the details, but use your imagination.

Mary was starting to freak out, and I said: "Mary, no worries, I know how to make drinks and tend bar. I did it in college. We'll be fine."

Mary said with a concerned voice: "OK, take off your coat and put on his jacket." So picture this, I am now wearing a yellow jacket with a white collar that is three sizes too small for me and a nametag that says "Bob".

Grandpa always said, "In life you have to play the cards you are dealt!" He also said, "It's a lot easier to ride a horse in the direction it's going."

At that moment, I am sure Grandpa Frank was looking down (or up) and laughing hysterically.

Well, the doors opened, and I poured stiff drinks at the open bar for 45 minutes, and these people drinking like they were going to the electric chair the next morning!

We had a good time making small talk and telling jokes, and I learned so much more about these folks in this short time. It is amazing what people will tell bartenders!

There was a tip jar on the corner of the bar, and I strategically placed three five-dollar bills in it hoping to inspire some generosity from these folks. (That was another lesson Grandpa taught me about human behavior!)

Just as they sat down for dinner, Bob came back, and since Mary had unleashed a tirade on Bob's boss about him, he was removed quietly and permanently from the room. (I never found out what really happened to him and never saw him again.)

Well, instead of sitting down to eat with everyone, I stayed at the bar, and my spot at the table with a place card holder with my name on it remained vacant. I enjoyed hearing the buzz through the room as folks wondered what happened to the after dinner speaker.

Many guests returned for a refill and more conversation at the bar in the back during dinner and, when they announced they would be closing the bar in 15 minutes, it was one last crush for doubles. These folks were not lightweights!

The emcee was noticeably nervous when he walked to the podium because he was under the impression there was no speaker. Mary said loudly so the whole group could hear, "the speaker is here, please start his introduction." I remained in the back of the room, removed the bartender jacket, replaced it with my suit coat, and as he started the last line of my introduction...

"And now please help me welcome, from Orlando, Florida, Captain Frank Candy." I threw my shoulders back and walked tall down the middle of the room.

You could have heard a pin drop. The only prop I was holding was the tip jar, and I placed it on the podium so everyone could see it.

The look on these people's faces was so funny. Just sheer confusion and disbelief.

For an opening line, I held up a glass of water that looked like vodka with a twist and said: "Cheers! People tell bartenders the darndest things."

Most of them laughed a nervous laugh as I explained how right before we opened the doors the bartender vanished so I offered to cover for him, and asked, "How did you like the bar service tonight?"

Well, these people thought that was pretty cool, and they hooted and hollered while I informed them that the sacred covenant for the patron and bartender relationship, like client-attorney privileges, was in place and everything they told me is confidential and will never be revealed. Again they laughed and there was a collective sigh of relief.

During my presentation I used this experience to emphasize how important it is to be a team player, to look for opportunities to show up and step up, and to be willing to serve in any capacity to create an experience that matters – and, when you can, to have a good time doing it like I did.

Then I made a joke about how, "Hopefully, the uniforms will fit you better." Everyone cracked up.

Now some of the things they told me reminded me of some experiences I had that they could relate to. This really touched their hearts and made a big difference in their overall experience that night.

I used some of these points and told a story about a homeless guy I had met while volunteering with a local church at the local homeless shelter.

He worked in the food service industry. His child became ill and then his wife became ill, and he had to take off work to care for them, so he was fired.

He got behind on his bills and rent, was evicted, and it was a slippery slope. They ended up living at the shelter.

Just about everyone in the homeless shelter has a story. And everyone wants a second chance, and most of the time a few bucks, another chance, and a decent opportunity is all they need to get started again. I know this because I was homeless at age 13 with my mom, and good people who were complete strangers reached out to us. It is a lesson I have never forgotten, and always look for ways to pay it forward.

Near the end, I asked: "Did you enjoy the speech tonight?"

They clapped and cheered, and Mary the meeting planner was smiling from ear to ear. So was the hotel's general manager and assistant managers, along with a couple hotel executives from the company who were standing in the back of the room.

Then I went on to say I could not accept the tip money tonight because I was paid for my services, and I was just volunteering as the bartender to participate in making the whole experience as good as I could.

Then I held up the tip jar and said: May I have your permission to give the money to the homeless shelter? They collectively said yes and I continued, "I am going to give this money to the home-less shelter tomorrow morning. But before I do, I am going to pass this around to each of you, and if you are so moved, how about looking deep into your hearts, and digging deep in your wallets, and putting a few bucks in there for those good people who need another chance."

What happened next was amazing. These generous people stuffed the jar with thousands of dollars, some even wrote checks. And then one man came up to me after and said he would match it, and he wrote a check too. It was a good day for the shelter and the people in it.

That night I invited Mary to come with me to drop it off in the morning. She confided that she had never been to a homeless shelter and had to be at the airport by 11 o'clock to check in and catch her flight. I said, "OK, let me pick you up in the morning. We will get breakfast, drop off the money at the shelter, and I will have you at the airport at 10:45. Guaranteed." She was still unsure and hesitant, mostly because she admitted later that it was fear of the unknown. So knowing she liked old cars, I gave her a choice of cool old cars I could pick her up in. She ended up choosing my old, Hot Rod Lincoln.

The next morning I met Mary at her hotel and we loaded up the car with her gear before taking her to breakfast and then the shelter. To make a long story short, Mary and I are still friends but this experience changed her life. Over time, her company outsourced her job to an independent planner and she was inspired to accept a job as an event planner for a group that raises money for the homeless. It's nice when things work out.

Look, as a speaker you never know how you can change lives and change the world, you just need to work on improving and getting better, and do your best, every time.

Mary went back to the agent at the speakers' bureau that booked me and raved all about what I'd done. Her company booked me for several events, and all those spin-off bookings all went back to the bureau.

Then the GM at the hotel called to ask me to deliver a talk about going the extra mile in service to his whole staff, all three shifts. It took two days. (But he did insist I leave out any mention of "Bob"!)

All these booking were referred to the bureau as spin-off business because I never would have gotten the work if they hadn't provided me with the original opportunity.

When our agents hear the same names of speakers or entertainers who did well over and over again, and the meeting planner raves about a speaker or entertainer, we know we want to explore the opportunity to work with them. Of course, it's also a good way to discover whom you don't want to work with.

Reputation counts for a great deal in the speaking and entertainment business.

An important part of being really good requires getting honest with yourself and knowing your capabilities, your limitations, and the audiences that are a great, good or poor fit for you.

While it is always prudent to avoid situations that are not the best for you and what you do, it is even more prudent to avoid them when a bureau is involved.

Never hesitate to politely turn down a bureau date if you feel, for any reason, the engagement would not be a good fit for you. It might be the topic, audience, schedule or travel requirements. The last thing you want is a booking with a bureau that does not go well. In our profession, the speaker is always in the spotlight; good or bad. When it goes well, the speaker gets the credit. If it does not go well, for any reason, the bureau and the agent will bear the burden of blame.

Even being good is not enough. It's just the start; merely a pre-requisite. Your talent and ability can be the cornerstone of a good relationship with any speaker bureau, but it takes many bricks and boards, cement and nails to complete the structure.

Summary: As a speaker, or performer, you never know how you can change lives and change the world, you just need to work on improving and getting better, and be in the moment, and do your best, every single time.

Your reputation counts, so take really good care of it.

CHAPTER 5

Be Real. Be Good. Be Patient. Be Ready.

Speakers need to be aware that once they start working with a bureau, the bookings are not going to pour in. It will take time.

Best practice: The Golden Rule.

Finding the perfect speaker and connecting them with the right client is a matchmaking process that requires much skill, blessed timing, and sometimes luck. Sometimes committees or task forces are involved, and so much of it is done over the phone and Internet. It can be challenging to hone in on the desires and risk tolerance of the decision makers.

Let's say a college quarterback rated very high in the college playoffs, and it has been his dream to play for the Green Bay Packers. However, right now the Packers have strength and depth in the quarterback position. What they really need are fullbacks and receivers, so they are not signing any quarterbacks at this time.

Even though the young man may be as good as they get, he has no chance of signing with the Packers, at least not right now.

Often, it's the same with speakers and entertainers. A very good speaker wants to work with a certain bureau, but at this time the bureau already has a good working relationship with several very good speakers who speak on the same topic. The speaker's chances of getting a starting position with this bureau are not good, at least not right now. The best the speaker can hope for is to perhaps get a seat on the bench, listed on the website, and then patiently wait for the situation to change.

When I was hoping for a chance to work with a bureau in New York, I was told, "Sorry, we checked you out, and we already have more speakers than we can book on the subjects you offer. No sense in taking on more talent and thinning our roster further."

During our conversation, I heard Frank Sinatra's music playing faintly in the background. We then chatted about Mr. Sinatra's music and career for a few minutes. After our conversation had ended, I sent a handwritten note thanking him for his consideration, good recommendations, and valuable time, I included a Limited Edition, Gold Disc of Frank Sinatra's first Duets album. The bureau director replied with a very nice thank you note.

Well, as luck would have it, I was booked over the next year by several tech clients that the New York bureau was bidding on. This came about because I delivered one great program for a company and the VP of Sales promoted me to his friends in the telecom business and we closed several deals. When the New York bureau followed up with their clients and heard over and over again they lost the business to me, they were both impressed and disappointed to lose the deals.

The New York bureau called me a year later and said, "We have a booking for you." That booking turned into three spin-offs, and it was the start of a good relationship. It's nice when things work out.

There is a ranking order at every speakers' bureau. Most of us have our favorite speakers, trainers and consultants.

Either formally or informally, the line-up at a speakers' bureau works much like the depth chart for a sports team. Baseball, football, basketball, hockey – pick one, it doesn't matter. Some players earn the opportunity to play on the first string; some are on the second string. Some are waiting on the bench and hoping for their chance.

At our bureau we have an established group of speakers that we are confident and comfortable with. They are our first string. We have a comfort level with them like our favorite chair and Grandma's recipes for apple pie. One word could describe that entire situation: TRUST.

When there is a call for a leadership expert, the first string gets the first opportunity. If the first person is booked, out of the budget or not a good fit for any other reason, the second string person gets the opportunity.

When a customer service expert who was the first stringer with a good bureau that booked many experts, wins the lottery and retires to a tropical island, all of the experts in that field move up a slot. Obviously that doesn't happen often!

Another bureau put "holds" on my calendar for several years, but no bookings. Then they asked me to fill in for a speaker who had a personal emergency (death in the family) and could not make the date. Geographically, I was closest, and since it was in Central Florida and a good fit for my topics, but not my normal fee, I still agreed to do it because, I thought, when might they call again and give me an opportunity? Since I had nothing on the calendar, I could easily drive to the engagement and I would not have to go through airport security. We agreed; I signed off on the paperwork and was booked for the client's event.

I prepared for nine hours the day before the event by customizing the content, rehearsing the speech, and modifying the multi-media presentation. Plus, I visited one of their locations about 40 miles away and took some pictures of it to include in my presentation.

The morning of the event while they were reading my introduction, the VP walks up to me backstage and tells me they just cut my time slot from 55 minutes to 25 minutes.

For most speakers, this is a nightmare.

However, luck favors the prepared person. I have a strategy for situations like that.

Well, it went by very quickly, and I had to wrap it up. So, near the end of the speech, I asked if they liked the presentation (dangerous move, because if you sucked you will be booed); however they cheered and shouted, so I very politely asked the audience to recommend they invite me back again, and proceeded to tell them all the great and cool stuff we could share next time. I closed with a powerful ending, and I planted the seed for more business and bookings.

Best practices: Never tell them what they missed, or give them the perception of being short-changed. Always leave them wanting more. That client has booked me through the same bureau several times, and the bureau has been booking me ever since.

In the call centers, we say: "Keep calling them, be nice, be understanding, and be polite. Stay in touch until they buy or die. Just be patient."

On many occasions, I have had speakers ask me, "What topic is hot? Can you book me if I speak on that topic?"

Delivering speeches to a group is like singing a song in concert, you better be really passionate about it, or you will sound like the Beach Boys playing and singing, *Help Me Rhonda* for the 24 thousandth time! It might be good to hear, but it lacks real passion.

Nothing against the Beach Boys, I like their music, please don't send me hate mail.

To get in the door with a bureau, they have to be in need of a speaker like you, to serve their clients, at this time. And remember, it is not the bureau who drives the market; it is the demand that drives and controls the market.

When you call a bureau, they will ask you: What is your brand? How do you position yourself in the marketplace? What is your specialty? Who is your best audience? What are your topics? Do you specialize in personal development or professional development? From where are you traveling? What is your fee? Do you customize your talks? What is your level of experience? How many full fee paid engagements have you booked in the last 12 months? These are all valid questions that identify you in terms of what their market demands are. Be ready to answer them.

What makes a speaker compelling? It could be the topic, style, or the speaker's background. It might be what the speaker lived through or accomplished. But the speaker must be clear on the answer. A way to gauge this: Do they have a concise 'elevator speech' about what they offer in thirty seconds or less?

Chances are, there are some bureaus that do not need you right now, and there are others who do. Some of the ones who do may even be looking for you, so you need to be easy to find.

How Most Speaker-Bureau Relationships Originate:

On behalf of a client: The bureau is looking for a speaker who does a good job with a specific topic or for a specific audience. Example: An attorney who delivers a presentation on wealth building and preservation for real estate investors. Another example: a former POW for a convention of veterans or defense contractors.

Recommendation by one of the bureau's clients: This is more customary when an agent, or the bureau the agent works for, has a deep and broad market penetration in a specific industry like high schools or colleges, or high-tech or low tech, agriculture, or government.

Recommendation by a trusted speaker who works with the bureau: This is peer-to-peer networking and most of the time it works. It has backfired when a prominent speaker delivers a talk at speakers' convention and declared from the stage, "You should work with a speakers' bureau." The audience members dutifully wrote that down and took action when they returned to their office.

The result? Our record was over 400 calls from speakers looking for representation in July of 2005, after a big convention for speakers.

Recommendation from another bureau: This is powerful and has an impact.

The bureau is losing dates to the speaker. When an agent loses multiple booking opportunities to another speaker, it makes them pay attention.

The last one on the list is the surest and quickest route through the door.

Best practice: Sell your services in the marketplace as effectively as you can. It is the surest way to build your brand, develop your reputation, and agents at bureaus will notice you.

Be patient, and be ready.

Speaking is a serious and highly competitive business. If a bureau is losing sales to you, it is going to track you down and ask for your media kit and video!

And if you can get a bureau that is booking you successfully to recommend you to other bureau's they co-broker with and trust, you have a better shot of moving the evaluation process along faster. Over the years, I have done this very selectively with our best speaker partners to our best bureau partners.

Strategy: Up and coming speakers should spend most of their time developing the best speech, the best performance, and the best products, and then market themselves to their local and regional market. If they are good, spin-off and referral business will grow, and the bureaus will come looking for them.

Dedicated athletes who are out of work and want to play will work on their game and conditioning every day, they still believe they have a chance to be on a team and contribute to the success of the team. They are committed to being the best every day.

They get up early; they workout hard; they study hard; they make good decisions, get plenty of rest, and get ready and stay ready, because when the phone rings and the coach is asking, "Do you want to play for our team?" – they better be ready.

Are you 100% ready when a bureau calls you to ask if you want an opportunity?

When you prepare and do your job well, sooner or later agents will contact you, and your turn will come.

Here is another misunderstood tip: Established speakers should send out unsolicited press kits and let the bureau know which speakers they precede or follow year after year.

Moment of truth: You should connect with a bureau first by communicating your brand and position in the market, and determining if there is mutual interest; then send your media kit if they request one and agree to look at it. I have watched established speakers earn awards or designations in the speaking industry and send out hundreds of expensive media kits, with very poor results.

Every week we receive many unrequested media kits and/or books sent to us from speakers looking for representation. About half the time there is a letter from a PR firm or the publisher, suggesting we should book this person based on the fact they wrote a book. This is one of the biggest wastes of money, paper, ink, postage and resources in the industry.

If you connect with them to determine there are mutual possibilities, then work on improving it. If you are a football player contacting basketball coaches... well, that's going nowhere. If you play classical piano, and you are contacting an agent that only books country bands, that's going nowhere too. If you are a popular author, and an admired speaker who is an expert on professional development, and you make contact with an agent at a bureau with corporate clients, then you are going in the right direction. Ding! Ding! Ding! Ca-Ching!

The meetings industry is market-driven as are most industries in a free economy. To become an in-demand player, you have to offer a valued service and be ready to respond effectively to the appeal of the market.

Summary: Be ready and be prepared for when an agent asks you:
What is your brand?
How do you position yourself in the marketplace?
Do you have a bureau / agent friendly media kit to send us?
What is your specialty?
Who is your best audience?
What are your topics?
Do you specialize in personal development or professional development?
Where do you live, and are you traveling from there?
What are your travel policies?
What is your fee?
Do you customize your shows or presentations?
What is your level of experience?
How many full fee paid engagements have you booked in the last 12 months? Who are the agents you are working with at this time?

These are all valid questions that identify you, brand you and position you, so far as market demands are concerned. The best practice is to always be ready to answer them.

CHAPTER 6

Be Bureau-Friendly - Walk the Talk

Being bureau-friendly in the speaking business is usually defined (by speakers) as leaving your contact information off your promotional material so the client cannot get in touch with you behind the bureau's back. This represents the disinformation and propaganda delivered by organizations that speakers chose to belong too.

Read this carefully: Being bureau-friendly is not about policy and procedure. It is about your business philosophy and attitude.

Working with a speakers' bureau is a business relationship, and all successful business relationships are built on trust, cooperation, and integrity.

When the philosophy and attitude are right, the policy and procedure are secondary. If the philosophy, attitude, or values are wrong, then the policy is worthless.

Client relationship management is a viewpoint, a philosophy, a mannerism, and an attitude that transcends the relationship.

The really important thing here is not so much what you put on the back of your brochure, but how you handle your business when it comes to bureaus. It's more important to honor obligations to bureaus than it is to leave your phone number off your media kit.

If you are booked for an event by an agent at a bureau, and if you think it's OK to invite the audience to visit your website that has your contact information on it, you are not bureau-friendly. The better way is to invite the audience members to visit the bureau's site with your biography, videos, and program details on it.

If you invite them to connect with you on social media or say: "Give us your email so we can invite you to join our mailing list", you are not bureau-friendly.

When you are on stage doing a bureau date, you represent the bureau. Period. You are an extension of the bureau's professional team, plus an integral part of their public relations efforts and marketing department.

On the day of the booking, you must remember that if you do well, everybody does well. If you fail to meet or exceed the expectations of the audience or client, you just set off a lingering stink bomb in the bureau's office, and that rotten egg, burnt hair, rancid garlic, old onion, awful ammonia smell rarely goes away!

If you have trouble deciding if a spin-off does or doesn't belong to the bureau, you are not bureau-friendly. If you would really rather book them all direct, you are not bureau-friendly.

Look, it's your choice. Most of life and business is about free will and choice. Why are some speakers able to work with bureaus, book 100% of their engagements, and keep their calendars full with clients they like? It's because they understand the bureau–agent–speaker relationship, and they honor it 100% of the time.

If your business philosophy is bureau-friendly, bureaus will know they can rely on you.

It will never be enough to tell them that you are bureau-friendly. You will have to show them. Walk the walk.

You should not do business with people who are not reliable. Neither should speakers' bureaus. Wisely, most bureaus are reluctant to stake the future of their business on speakers with questionable attitudes about the legitimacy of bureaus in the industry.

Many speakers recognize speakers' bureaus as premium level customers. A good relationship with a bureau can yield multiple dates per year. Good customers should expect honesty and fairness, and to be treated with respect.

Good customers who are frequent buyers deserve a discount. A bureau's commission is really a deal if they book you and do the work they should do.

Commissions to bureaus are like retailers being able to buy wholesale because they buy in volume. They are like the multiple discounts you get when you buy your brochures in larger lots. You might even think of them as frequent flyer points and free upgrades; something someone earns by being a premium-level customer.

Look at it this way: Bureaus are premium-level customers. A bureau that books you twenty or thirty times a year can make a big difference in your annual gross.

A bureau that is willing to recommend you often and book you every month out of the year deserves…what? How about a holiday card, a thank you note, a thoughtful gift or an occasional call from the speaker?

Recently a speaker sent us a bottle of the cheapest sparkling wine known to mankind. Seriously, the bulk rate postage cost more than the wine. And, since I rarely drink, nor do the people in our office drink, the impact was not a positive one.

In our office, we like doing business with good clients. We especially like doing business with premium-level clients who put several or a dozen dates on the calendar in a given year. We always make sure to show our appreciation for their loyalty.

Back in the 1990's I received a call from a man in a small town in Pennsylvania, not far from Pittsburgh. He was inquiring about booking me for his Chamber of Commerce because he had heard I would be speaking to a hospital group in Pittsburgh soon.

I asked him how he heard about me. He said he recognized my name because he found my book in a barbershop in Beaver Falls, PA and had read it. Inside it was my brochure, which had a bureau label.

But, instead of calling the bureau, he said he just called the publisher of the book who gave him my direct number. I learned his name was Charlie, and I explained to Charlie that I would need all the important information, the proper spelling of his full name, and his phone number, plus details on the event, date, time, location, etc., then he could expect a call from the agent from the bureau to make all the arrangements.

Best practice: When my bureau gets a direct call from a meeting planner inquiring about a speaker, we start out by learning why we got the call. We find out where the meeting planner received the referral, heard them speak, or how they came by the name.

In 1999, a man in Texas said he got my name as a referral from his partner, who said one of his customers in Tampa (I live in Florida), sent him the video link. The guy in Tampa said a JV Partner from Cleveland gave it to him (I was born in Cleveland). That guy said he got it from a friend at a technology group that saw me deliver a keynote speech for Texas Instruments in Las Vegas a long time ago. And *that* guy was the cousin of my college roommate. So we booked that one direct.

If there is a bureau involved, we will find out. When we do, we explain how it works to the client, and put the bureau on the booking. Usually we'll say something to the meeting planner like: "Joe Jones is the one who will handle this booking and put this on Frank's schedule. Let me have your full name and number, plus all the details, so I can have Joe get in touch with you ASAP."

At that point, I have the expectation of the bureau earning a commission by making the sale and doing the work.

We have made mistakes. When we do, we are quick to admit them. One of my mentors, a manager who trained me on technology, taught me to run towards a problem. He said it would never get better, and he is right. So go after it, handle it, and move on.

On more than one occasion, I have paid two commissions on the same engagement. It was the right thing to do, because I had already paid a commission to the wrong bureau, and it would damage the long-term relationship. So, I just sucked it up and paid both.

Bureau Number One had sent out a catalog that I was listed in, to a national management group with chapters all over the country.

Well, this woman called to book a date with Bureau Number One for this chapter. I get a call from Bureau Number One, confirmed the date was available and it was a good fit, and put a hold on the calendar. All this was standard procedure.

Then, a few months later, in a pre-conference call when I am speaking to the client, she tells me she left the power company and now has a new job. She saw me speak at the power company's annual meeting (where I'd been booked by Bureau Number Two). She said I had done a very nice job and was excited to have me speak at this event. I thanked her for the compliment, her vote of confidence, and the opportunity, and then we wrapped up the call.

Fair is fair, I own and run a bureau and know the rules. It's like living in a glass house. So, I called the owner of Bureau Number Two, informed them of the situation, and told them they could expect a check for the full commission tomorrow via FedEx. Mea Culpa. Everything was understood, transparent, and there was no damage to the relationship.

- When a speaker voluntarily calls to tell us about a lead for a spin-off opportunity -
- When a speaker calls our bureau after the program to give use feedback, and give me leads -
- When they voluntarily give out our contact information, and business cards, -
- When I know their office team inquires to qualify incoming direct calls to see where it originated –
- When they tell the client to call our bureau for referrals of other speakers –

That tells me what I need to know about the speaker's business philosophy, attitude, and trustworthiness, and I know that speaker is bureau-friendly.

Friendly business is a two-way street. The bureau that recognizes you as bureau-friendly will be speaker-friendly to you.

From time to time, some speaker will call and ask, "How long should I be expected to protect a bureau on a spin-off? Is it one year, two, or three?"

When I hear that, I know the speaker is stuck on policy and hasn't caught on to the right philosophy that builds business relationships.

W. Mitchell, CPAE, said to me over 25 years ago, "In my world, spin-off business is for life." That's bureau-friendly.

On the other hand, when I received a call from a very good client who has been booking with us for over a decade, and they tell me they are receiving annoying calls from a magician's office manager we booked him two years and one week ago, and this person is asking to book him again, but directly, and the client tells me in very clear terms that our bureau is on the verge of losing her business unless the annoying calls from the magician's office stop, I'm not happy.

With a little digging we find out the magician has instructed his office to call every client we have booked him for to try to book him direct. That was the start of the end of what would and should have been a long and valuable relationship.

Over the years, we have booked many, many speakers, and a low majority has been truly bureau-friendly. Some big names that you would recognize have been busted on this. They usually blame their staff. One even blamed his wife who works in his office! (Man, did that come back to bite him in the butt! I bet he called 911 and yelled, "Help I'm bleeding!")

The people who trust us and assist us will make money with us. How long can they expect us to honor their spin-offs? Until somebody is singing *Amazing Grace* at my memorial service.

Summary: Developing a bureau-friendly viewpoint, philosophy, manor, and attitude, will fill your calendar with bookings and show up on your bottom line every year, in a big way, for a long, long, time.

CHAPTER 7

Be Known - Stairway to Heaven

Speakers who are good at what they do become more and more in demand as they become better known, even iconic. Demand is a by-product of fame. Fortunately, in professional speaking you do not have to be famous. You do need to be known by as many of the key players in the industry as possible. Being known by the bureaus is a very good thing.

If your name is a household word, you might be famous; you might become so popular you need a full-time personal manager and/or agent to manage the flow of work for you. There is a difference.

The main one is this: Your agent would be out getting business for you as his/her employer. Agents at bureaus, on the other hand, work for meeting planners. I know this gets confusing, but "the agent" can play many roles.

A famous general, who was given credit for leading an army that won a war, was getting thousands of requests for speaking engagements and personal appearances after he retired. He needed more than one full-time agent to handle and process the flow of calls and opportunities.

A famous college football coach, who won national championships, was receiving over 500 requests a year for speaking engagements. He only wanted to limit the times he would and could speak to about forty engagements per year, and they had to be in the off-season. He needed a full-time agent to manage this for him.

While it is nice to be a famous celebrity, the marketing of a professional speaker needs a different plan. There is no one plan that fits everyone. There are many books dedicated to marketing professional services. My next book will be a very detailed explanation of this, so keep an eye out for it. Please check the website for a list of book I recommend. http://www.publicspeakingformoney.com

You need to brand yourself and your company. You need to have a tested and proven marketing plan that works and positions you in the right places at the right time, and you need the right credentials and tools to make it happen. It's unlikely that an agent or bureau will represent you or be able to sell you without it.

There are people who believe membership in the National Speakers Association (often referred to as NSA) is important. They say it is a good place to get to know the players in the industry. It's also a good place to get known. There is some truth to this, and I was a member for over 20 years. Some of the best friends I have today I met through NSA. NOTE: They are proposing a name change so stay tuned.

But, like every professional association, it has its pros, cons, and limitations, and NSA, like many other organizations is not for everyone.

In the past, some agents and bureaus claimed they will only book members of NSA. When you make contact with agents, you may wish to bring this up and get it out in the open.

Please evaluate memberships in any professional association carefully. Your investment of time and money is not unlimited. It is not the right thing for everybody.

About ten years ago, I was speaking with a professional meeting planner from a billion dollar company. It was our first encounter. She was inquiring about three speakers we represented.

Regretfully, I mentioned one of them was a member of NSA and had their professional certification. Well, she ripped into me because she had hired a speaker with the NSA "CSP" certification once and they bombed. It was so bad that she almost lost her job over it and was passed over for a promotion. Ouch.

Perhaps the speaker had a bad day; it happens. Nobody is perfect. I don't know the details, and I won't judge or criticize because I too had a couple "less than up to my high standards" programs along my journey.

Along the way, I had to mediate some adverse post-event situations that we booked and involved some of the best speakers in the world.

Things happen; we are all human. But when bad things happen, my philosophy and process is this:

1. Listen to everyone carefully, and get all the facts.
2. Ask and look for fair solutions that work.
3. Don't throw anyone under the bus.
4. Be willing to eat humble pie, lots and lots of humble pie. Like 10,000 calories or more.
5. Be prepared to return the money, write letters of apology, offer to call the offended parties, and offer up many mea culpa's to them. Do what it takes to make it right.

6. If you are a speaker, or entertainer, and the client wasn't happy with your speech or performance, and you believe a full or partial refund is due, then be sure to compensate the agent and bureau, because this has taken up their time and expertise. It most likely costs them a client, which in the big picture is worth many thousands of dollars.

Think about this – the blown engagement was a one-hour or one-day event in your life and career. Making it go away quickly and quietly is in everyone's best interest.

Saving your relationship with an agent and the bureau, and your reputation in the industry should be a very high priority for you. In the long run, the agent and bureau relationship is worth many, many, many dollars.

Hiring lawyers, filing lawsuits, going to depositions and hearings, filing motions and getting tied up in court for years and years benefits nobody, except the lawyers who are looking to buy a new car or vacation home.

The title of this chapter is "Stairway to Heaven, Be Known." Choosing the legal route is the express elevator to hell, and the wrong things to be known for. Years ago Madonna said, "There is no such thing as bad publicity." In this case, one might conclude that Madonna was wrong; there are certain things like this scenario; that are just bad publicity.

Any speaker who says he or she never delivered a less than acceptable program will probably lie about other stuff too. (This is just my opinion; don't send me hate mail!)

This is a good time to mention that the reason I chose this business is because of so many great people who work in it. For each story I share about a problem, there are thousands that worked very well and were successful. It is a very low percentage of problems. Heck, if I could play golf that well, I would be on the Senior Golf Tour.

Today, in corporations and trade associations, it is a common practice to spread out the responsibility for the choice of who gets booked by sending recommendations to a committee who then review the profile of many speakers. They narrow it down; sometimes interview each candidate by phone, vote on their favorites, and then book the winning speaker(s) for their big conference.

Here is a case study on how this works - sometimes.

Here is a scenario happening now and will continue to happen in the future.

The 74-year-old Chairman of the Board, the 60-year-old Baby-Boomer CEO, the 55-year-old President, and several Sr. VP's ranging in ages from 60's to 40's are in a board meeting in the Ivory Tower. Got the picture?

The Chairman, Charles, says: "Sales have been dreadful, morale among the sales force is very low, we need to pump up our people. Let's have a sales meeting at the Sands in Las Vegas at the end of September. Sergio, you're the Sales VP so you know all about motivational and inspirational speakers... Get us some good speakers. Harrumph harrumph."

Sergio excuses himself, goes to the outer office, and tells the executive assistant, Susan, to contact his secretary, Stevie, and tell her to find speakers for the sales meeting in September. Susan does as instructed via email or phone to Stevie, who then forwards the message to her assistant, Sharron, who in turn delegates the task to a temp worker named Sam.

By now, the information has gone through several layers of interpretation and communication, and, who knows, might be a bit convoluted. Then Sam passes it on to a student intern who lives in a cubical in the basement with Internet access and a laptop. His name is Simon. He's from the millennial generation, prefers texting to talking on the phone, and wears his ball cap backwards all the time.

Simon is very bright, computer literate, and a gamer with little experience in the real business world. He is being paid very little or nothing for this experience in corporate life. He reviews the request and his first interpretation is "Are these speakers like woofers and tweeters, man?" Now we are playing the guessing game, *Simon Says*.

Once Simon gets on track, he is now looking for speakers or trainers, and he discovers some of these speakers make more in one or two hours or days than he does in a year.

This makes his head shake and rattle loudly. Simon is the first gatekeeper in the process of discovering, identifying, qualifying, evaluating, and recommending professional speakers or trainers for the event. Is this right? Is this fair? Is life fair? Get real!

How good, how clear, how powerful is your marketing that it will make it through the evaluation process from Simon, Susie, Sharron, and Sam, all the way up to the big decision makers like Charlie and the CEO in the "C" suite of the ivory tower?

This is the billion-dollar question we are facing: How does your media kit and video get the attention of, and sell you to, four generations in the workforce?

Answer that question and you will be rich.

Now do you have a clearer picture of why you need professionals to assist you in developing your brand, media kit, promotion materials, and demo videos? Do what you do best; outsource the rest.

Moment of Truth: Be really good at what you do, so good you become known for it, and be true to yourself. You cannot please everybody. If you spend your life trying to make everyone happy, it will be a long and difficult journey.

Summary: Being a famous celebrity or media icon is desirable, and it will create demand for you; but keeping it going at any level requires a good plan and you working your plan. Essentially, bureau and agents are in the marketing business, and speakers are chosen based on certain factors including popularity, topic, reputation, and authenticity. The more you know about how to do it well and do it efficiently, the more it will increase your bottom line.

CHAPTER 8

The First Kiss. The Secret. The Priceless Plan.
The Script That Works
How to Make Contact With Agents and Bureaus.

Should you call and ask permission to send a press kit?

Sure, but it would be better if you called to determine if it might be a good fit for you, and what you offer. Here is a good phone script. Be prepared to have the following information ready:

Hello, My name is, _____,

Is this a good time to talk for a minute?

I have been speaking professionally for ___ years.

The topic(s) I address are _____.

My best clients are _____ Be specific. (Manufacturing, banks, construction, energy, transportation, sales, management, engineers, schools, government, local, national, international, etc.)

My fee range is _____.

Do you believe what I have to offer may be a good fit for you client list?

Now, this is important and combines common sense and common courtesy with Cold calling 101".

When you call, the odds are good you will be speaking to a receptionist with little or no power or authority to assist you. So be very polite. Start out by asking if this is a good time to talk for a minute? He or she may be on two other lines, have three people staring at them in the lobby, and a couple more waiting for him or her to guide them to a conference room or an agent's office.

If they say no, ask: "When would be a better time to call back?" I have heard everything from 5 or 10 minutes, to tomorrow morning or afternoon, to next week, to never.

Yep, a few times in the last 20 plus years I have actually heard "never".

This really bothered me because I thought I had done or said something insensitive. It turns out in one case the company just announced it was closing and the phone line was dead when I called back a few days later and I later read about it in the business journal. In another case, I said, "May I ask why not?" and I was told they were going to be bought out and the new boss was passing out pink slips on Friday.

We move forward.

If he or she says yes, then ask who would be the right person to discuss representation for new speakers or talent, get the proper pronunciation and spelling of their names, and ask if they are available.

If you get on the phone with the right person, go through the same routine: Is this a good time for you to talk for a few minutes?

There is a 50-50 chance they will say, "Yes go ahead." Then go through your phone script from above.

Please don't be offended if they stop you part way through it and say they are not interested. They might get 10 or 20 calls a day like this, and either they stopped because they heard something like, "I speak at schools and churches", or "I speak for free and I want to get paid", or "I talk about my grandma's banana bread recipes"...or "How I overcame some human weakness like drinking or smoking, and I want to tell my story."

PLEASE do not interpret this as me being judgmental here; I just want you to understand there are over 1,000 speaker bureaus and thousands of agents out there.

Your time and their time are extremely valuable, and time is money.

For you, finding the right agent by phone is like dialing for dollars, and you need to get to the point quickly. The agents are looking for just the right combination for their roster. If what you are saying does not hit the hot buttons, just say "thank you" and move on.

If you call and say 'I offer programs on personal development and goal setting,' and the bureau has no clients who request those topics, it's not a fit. You would not call the Chevy dealer and ask for Ford parts. It's not the right fit. If you were looking for Ford parts, you would call the Ford Dealer. So keep calling until you find the right people with the right combination for you.

When you use this phone script you can contact a hundred or more per day, and you will narrow it down pretty quickly as to who is a good fit for you.

Just be ready to act; give them what they want, and how they want it, quickly.

You cannot push or force your way in the front door at a speakers' bureau. Word of your good work should precede you, delivered by other speakers, meeting planners, and even other bureaus.

Several years ago, one speaker, a speaker, kept calling and sending stuff. His reputation preceded him: a bad business deal he took part in left an old partner of mine attached to another object by an incline plane wrapped helically around an axis. In other words, he was screwed! I remembered it and filed it away.

Now I was always cordial to him, but cautious with him. One day, he calls up and announces that he is in town, and is coming over to our office to visit with our staff in one hour. I said, "Sorry, not today."

He said, "Hey, I am trying to build a relationship here."

Then I said: "I appreciate that, but we are very busy. We have appointments and conference calls scheduled with clients, and we are not going to drop everything which includes pre-scheduled meetings with clients who pay us money to book speakers and entertainers at the last minute just because you are here now. Next time, please call in advance and make an appointment."

In hindsight, I have no regrets. My team would not have liked his pushy style and machismo attitude, it would have damaged our good energy and momentum for the day and possibly longer. I focus on the best ways to protect our people, energy, and culture.

Eventually, I was invited to watch him deliver a program for a couple thousand people with a big company, at an international event. He bombed. Just ten minutes after he started his presentation, people were walking out and not coming back. When I stepped out to use the restroom, there were people in the hallway drinking coffee and grumbling about the speaker.

This speaker admitted to me afterwards it was not his best performance because he was not prepared. I made an attempt to offer constructive feedback and rudely was blown off, and treated very unprofessionally. We could never recommend him to a client in good faith. His failure to prepare and failure to be professional cost him millions of dollars.

Two important things here: If you think someone's blog post or story is about you, truth is it probably isn't, but you probably see yourself in it. Here's a suggestion...don't get upset with the mirror...fix the reflection.

By comparison to the speaker mentioned above, the next five speakers we traveled to watch deliver a presentation were very good, very professional, and we are working with four out of five of them. The fifth one met the man of her dreams and he proposed. They were married, she retired from speaking, and now they travel the world on his yacht. It's nice when things work out.

If a speaker has an event that is in their city or close to it, and if they booked through their own office, it's wise to invite bureaus to experience the speaker's live performance.

In turn, the bureau might ask if they can bring a meeting planner to watch them work.

But first, let me recommended that the speaker look up the location of the event's venue to determine if it is close or a reasonable distance. I remember a secretary in a speaker's office calling us to invite us to watch a speaker. We became excited, as we had been hoping to see this person live for over a year.

Well, she called and was all excited because the speaker was going to be delivering a program in Key Largo, Florida. That's a one-way, six-hour car trip for us from Orlando. Really? We had to inform her it would not work. Anybody could look on a map or the Internet and figure it out in under a minute.

Best Practice: Don't waste the agent's valuable time. They don't appreciate it.

The first thing a speaker must do is get the client's permission to invite agents or other people to the show. If it's granted, then follow-up and confirm the opportunity.

Is it close? How close? Then, if it seems reasonable, give them a call and ask them if they would like an invitation to attend the event.

Warning here: We had a very nice speaker I had booked for corporate events coming through Orlando. He was speaking at a church for free and selling his books and audio programs. He invited our people to watch him at the church. Now, I had known this speaker since the '70's, seen him in the past, and booked him because he was very good for corporate sales events and motivational keynotes.

Two of our agents went to the church and enjoyed his presentation, but in our Monday morning meeting told me they could not see how he would be a good speaker for a corporate meeting. What they witnessed was a spiritual presentation about personal development, and they could not make the mental leap necessary to envision him working a large corporate event.

Lesson: Perception is reality. The speaker had the best of intentions by making the invitation, but it failed to achieve the desired results.

As my Uncle Joe used to say, "You don't show a guy who wants to buy a sports car a truck."

In the late '90's, I made the same mistake with an agent in the mid-west. I invited them to watch me deliver a program on trade-show marketing, but it was the fifth program I had been hired to deliver for the client and not my core topic or close to my brand I am known for.

After the program, I introduced the agent to the meeting planner who shared with them about the good relationship they had from working with me for several years, and showed her the very good evaluations from the audience.

First impressions last a long time, and perception is reality. I never got a booking from the agent because they did not make the mental leap from tradeshow marketing to leadership, teamwork, and sales.

Before you make a recommendation, think about the strategy and desired results. Be sure you are ready to provide them with as much information as they need about the event and the client.

If it was an event booked by a speakers' bureau partner, the first call a speaker should make is to the agent to ask permission from the bureau and the client to invite someone and get their approval.

All the details are out in the open and transparent. By the way, I am batting about 25% – 75% with this approach. Meaning, 75% of the bureaus said: Sure, no problem; clear it with the client, and tell the other bureau we said hello.

The other bureaus were unwilling to allow the opportunity to move forward. It's their client; they are the boss, and in every case, they were understanding of the situation, grateful we brought it to them, but they declined.

Remember, it is their show, their client, and their rules. Now, if we had gone to the other bureau first to see if they were willing to show up, and then called the client and received permission, and then called the bureau who book it, and they declined, can you see the problems and issues raised? That is not being bureau-friendly, or a good bureau partner.

Here's how I do it: If a speaker gets approval to invite one of our agents, or myself, to watch them at an event another bureau booked, I will personally call the bureau owner and talk with them directly about the client and the speaker. Plus, I offer any assistance since I will be there.

When I show up, I am like a fly on the wall. I do not drink their water or coffee, eat their food, or do networking of any kind. I leave my business cards in the car. If anyone asks, I am just a friend of the speaker. Most of the agents I know operate the same way.

I would say more than 75% of the time, the other bureau owner asks me to call them to discuss my experience with the speaker and the event.

Next, if I invite an agent to watch me work, I offer to cover the agent's expenses, fuel, parking, tolls, mileage, and any other expenses they incur. It's not going to cost you or me much, but it shows you are aware of it and respectful for their time and resources. I never let them reach in their wallet for anything.

When you invite an agent to watch you deliver a presentation, agree to meet with them briefly before your presentation, make them feel welcome and comfortable, don't grill them with a bunch of questions. Agree to meet with them afterwards to connect again, and sit down and ask them for feedback and listen carefully. They probably have something valuable, and relevant to share with you.

On some occasions, I've had speakers call to ask how much I would charge to consult with them, and this included paying me to attend the event they were presenting a program. I am usually willing to invest about 10 to 20 minutes of my time on the front end to determine if it is a good fit, and there is the possibility of a long-term potential relationship to book them in the future.

Otherwise, I will probably be accepting money from someone I will probably have to reject for representation, and that doesn't end well.

Here's another thing that makes me (and other agents) crazy: Speakers or their assistants call or email to say, "I am speaking in Florida tomorrow, or the day after tomorrow, will you come watch me or them?" Really? How long ago did you confirm this booking? When did you book the travel? Couldn't you have called a few weeks or months in advance? How about giving us the opportunity to clear our schedules, get the right people lined up, etc.?

In one meeting with a group of about 15 agents from around the country, one of them brought this up and, Man, talk about pushing the big, red, pissed-off button hard. That unleashed a flood of bitterness in the meeting.

Conclusion? Don't do it. It's not a good way to connect with an agent. It is disrespectful and a waste of time. It shows a lack of professionalism, planning, and common sense.

We are based in Orlando, Florida. I have people call us to say: "My boss is speaking in Miami, can you watch him or her work? Is Orlando close to Miami?"

Seriously? We don't even know who these people are or what they speak about, and they are asking us to arrange for a 500 mile round trip. The cost for fuel, mileage, meals, and lodging, plus, highway tolls, are over $400.00.

Our policy now is a simple one, we politely explain that we do not agree to travel anywhere, to watch anyone, until we have reviewed his or her media kit, watched his or her video, and completed the due diligence required to consider representation. That's being fair to everyone.

Many meeting planners have turned to speakers bureaus to save time and money in the pursuit of good speakers for meetings and events.

Some companies have even turned to out-sourcing for meeting planners. This practice is on a steady growth curve.

It is not uncommon today for a speaker to be hired through a bureau, by an independent meeting planner, or DMC (Destination Management Company), or production company, on contract with an association, corporation, or other organization.

More speaking dates are being booked by bureaus. Many speakers who shunned bureaus in the past are rethinking that position and now seeking bureau relationships.

Some speakers who were very vocal and negative about bureaus are finding it difficult to break through the negative barriers they created.

Best Practices: On your way up the ladder in your career be nice to the people who helped you along the way, and the ones who matter. Now that I am considered one of the senior members of the profession, it has been interesting to watch the people who rose up the ranks and treated some of my good friends in the business poorly. Then the economy crashed, and they were coming back to us looking for work.

Simple mathematics will lead you to the correct assumption that it is easier to become known by a dozen or so speakers bureaus than it is to become known by several thousand meeting planners. A dozen good bureau contacts can easily lead to bookings with hundreds and thousands of meeting planners.

For this reason, the great majority of speakers' marketing efforts over the years have been directed to the bureaus. This has given speakers great leverage to their marketing efforts and marketing budgets.

One Bureau Leads to Many New Customers

Again, do the math. It is much more cost effective to reach the masses of meeting planners through speakers' bureaus. A successful marketing campaign to one meeting planner gives you one new customer. One times one equals one. A successful campaign to build a relationship with one bureau gives you many new opportunities with clients. One times many equals many, and in the speaking business, given the importance of spin-offs, many leads to many more.

There is one simple rule for marketing to speaker bureaus. It is the same rule that applies to all business marketing. It all has to be built around the wants and needs of the people you hope to serve, the bureau and their clients.

To put it simply – it's not about you; it is about them. All correspondence, phone calls, e-mails, newsletters, fax transmissions, visits...everything must be relevant to their interests and respectful of their time.

Before you call a bureau on the phone, remember how many times you have hung up on telemarketers. Always have a valid business reason for making contact. A purpose that appeals to the bureau's interest.

In relationships with all customers, it is about them, not you. Bureaus do not serve speakers. Bureaus serve meeting planners. In the meetings industry, all the money comes from those who hold the meetings, and they book the speakers, sign the contracts, and write the checks.

Do your homework. Find out when is the best time to call customers. Some bureau reps prefer to be called in the afternoon. Others would prefer for you to call in the morning. Some prefer evenings or weekends. When you do call, keep it short. The people who work at speakers bureaus make their living talking to their clients over the phone, not speakers.

A bureau rep's phone time is precious. It's better for them, and for you, for them to be on the phone with a prospect than it is for them to be on the phone with you. They are very much aware of this, and most of them wish speakers were more sensitive to this fact.

Most bureau reps prefer to correspond by e-mail because it's far less intrusive of their valuable time. Plus, they can multi-task and have a record of the communication.

It's Not What You Know...

Who you know is most important. Who you know is their "fame". How you know them is their "reputation". The important thing is who knows you, and how they know you. When you are known, and known in a good way, by a number of speakers' bureaus, your bookings, business, and bottom line will increase.

Most established speakers will tell you the best way to get known in this profession is to speak as often as you can, as well as you can. When a speaker is out in the marketplace doing a good job, word gets around quickly.

When compared to other professions and other industries, the speaking profession and the meetings industry is a small community. There are only a hundred thousand speakers, just over a thousand speakers bureaus, and there are not many meeting planners when you compare their numbers to other endeavors. The whole bunch of us together would barely populate a small town. News (good or bad) spreads fast in small towns.

Summary: Making contact with agents and speaker bureaus requires a good plan, understanding of the business, and developing a relationship. If done right that relationship is worth hundreds of thousands of dollars to you.

CHAPTER 9

Be Easy to Work With
Gotta Serve Somebody

It is commonly known among agents and representatives: If the process of working with a speaker or their office is difficult for whatever reason, we will avoid recommending them in the future.

We Are All in Sales and Service Now and Forever.

Being known as someone who is easy to work with is very important in bureau relationships.

First off, the bureau is your client, and clients prefer to work with those who give good service.

Secondly, it is in the bureau's best interest to send their clients speakers who understand service and are easy to work with.

Here's my favorite definition of "customer service": Making it easy for your customers to do business with you."

The soft drink industry experienced tremendous growth when the vending machine was introduced in the 1940's because it made it easy for customers to buy the products.

The same was true with the bottled water industry.

The auto industry took off when Ford created the assembly line, which lowered the price for the common man to buy one. Then General Motors offered different colors and their sales took off. Then, when automatic transmissions came along, it made them easier to drive, and sales increased again.

Computer sales exploded when Microsoft, HP, Compact, IBM, and Dell appeared on the scene and made computers cheaper and easier to use. Then Apple created a different business model of great experience and great service, at a higher price, which proved that people will pay for that experience.

Being user-friendly is a good strategy for any industry, business, or profession. You can be user-friendly by making it easy for people to do business with you.

In all business relationships, it pays to be flexible to the customer's way of doing things.

Expecting all bureaus to do everything the same way as all the other bureaus is like expecting all of the car manufacturers in the world to make the same vehicle with interchangeable parts.

Unless you run a government agency that people *must* deal with (like Social Security or the Department of Motor Vehicles), your customers will not do it your way. At the DMV you have to do it their way, and you know how popular they are.

The typical bureau corresponds differently, bills differently, pays differently, and in general does business differently than other bureaus. Over 35 years ago, the bureaus started conversations about standardization of contracts, rules, guidelines and policies. We made some good progress on some of them.

Like other customers, they have different needs, interest, backgrounds, and perspectives. Pick the ones you like, the people you are compatible and share the same values with, and go for the ride.

Customers Expect You to Do It Their Way

Some bureaus bill the client for expense reimbursement while some will expect the speaker to do that. Some will have the client pay you on site. Others will bill the client after the date. Some bureaus expect you to call the client as soon as the date is booked, others would prefer you never call the client.

If you cannot adapt to the way a bureau wants to do business, do not expect them to do business with you. In a free market customers dictate the format. If you don't want to do it his or her way, someone else will.

You are in business to make money, not to make a statement. It is better to be passionate about your topic than to be stubborn about how you do business. There is a rumor that those who speak for a living are over-blessed with ego. As a speaker or entertainer, you can help dispel this nonsense by being easy to work with.

For over 25 years, I have kept a written record in the form of a spreadsheet of how each bureau prefers to handle various things. That way we all have access to it in the system and can change it or update it quickly. To reap the great potential of bureau business, you have to make it easy for both bureaus and their clients to do business with you.

In our case, we request our speaker's call the client right after the program is booked. Usually we request that they contact them in the same week we send them the contract to lock in the date. If for no other reason than to touch base, reassure the client that we are all on track, say thank you for the opportunity, and set a time for a pre-conference call. That one added touch goes a long way in the relationship.

When we make an appointment for a pre-conference call, I like to offer a checklist to both parties, especially if it is a new meeting or event planner. Note: I just offer, I don't insist.

This list includes: discuss content, schedule, timing, flow, travel details, and confirm lodging and transportation, and more. Plus, if the program can be customized to the client's unique needs, that is a whole new list of questions.

After the event, if a client tells me this is one of the best speakers they have ever booked, and the speaker was easy to work with, then I know I have made a perfect match with the client and speaker.

"Most bureaus never release holds."

This is a common complaint from speakers. You hear them say things like, "The bureau put a hold on my calendar, and they never let me know what happened."

So what? Have you ever called a car dealer back to tell them you decided not to buy the car you test drove? Did you call up the resort to inquire about lodging details, and then call them back to inform them you decided not to take a vacation after all?

A hold is not a confirmed reservation. A hold simply means someone is thinking about hiring you and that you are in the running for a date, probably along with several other speakers.

A hold on your calendar does not mean that you might work the meeting planner into your schedule; it means the meeting planner might work you into their program. You hold the date as a courtesy to the client, giving them the right of first refusal. If no one else calls wanting to book the date, the fact that the hold is still there is a moot point.

Should you get another client interested in the date and make a firm offer, then you will be the one calling the bureau to give them twenty-four hour notice. Honor the holds you get from a bureau. If they evaporate, forget about it.

When a bureau does not call to release a hold, it usually means one of several things:

- The client booked some other speaker.
- The client used another bureau and booked some other speaker.
- The meeting was canceled.
- They decided not to hire a speaker.

Over fifteen years ago, this was a highly debated topic at the annual National Speakers Association Convention and the annual meeting for The International Association of Speakers Bureaus. Our leadership team at our speakers' bureau came up with a brilliant idea that has served us well.

When a client asks our bureau for a proposal, we identify and confirm the best speakers for the opportunity. We then confirm their availability, compatibility, and develop a cost analysis to deliver to the client in the form of a detailed proposal.

We ask each speaker to hold the date for a set period of time. Two weeks or one month is usually our plan. We say to the speaker, "If you have not heard back from us to set up a phone conference with the client, book the date, or extend the hold by this date then assume it is not going to happen and take it off your holds calendar."

The added value of this is that it gives you a valid reason to connect with the client to gently request updates in the decision-making process.

When someone from our bureau calls a speaker and asks them to put a hold on a date, I require our people to provide the date, time, city, organization, and the contact name. So the call goes like this.

On August 15th, I call one of the speakers we want to include in our proposal.

Ring, Ring, Johnny Speaker says: Hello?

Frank: Hi Johnny, Frank with American Speakers Bureau, is this is a good time for you to discuss a booking?

Note: 99% of the time Johnny says, "Hell yes!" or words to that effect.

Frank: Please check your calendar for December 1 or 2 in Florida.

Johnny: Looks like I am available, tell me more.

Frank: The client is having a two-day meeting. They are considering several options for a couple slots. They are a small group of about 150 managers, 50/50 male and female, between 35 and up to 60 years old. They want to be inspired by an interactive keynote. They like outdoor sports, and they want a one-hour presentation at 9 in the morning. Is it a good fit for you?

Johnny: Great fit for me, put me in coach.

Frank: OK, please write this down: The client is Tom Wilson, from Wilson Industries. The date, as I said, is December 1 or 2 in South Beach. If they book you, they want you to stay around for the parties and mingle with the group. They have enough in the budget for your full fee and all expenses for two nights.

Johnny: That sounds great; I would rather be in South Florida at the beginning of December than North East Ohio!

Frank: Excellent, please keep it on your calendar for four weeks. We will call you back if you get the booking, or if you make the cut and they need more time to make a decision. If you have not heard back from us by September 15, take the hold off your calendar and consider it dead. Do you have any questions for me?

Johnny: Not at this time, thanks for thinking of me.

Frank: Thank you Johnny, I wish you well! Bye-bye - Click

This strategy, and now our policy, is a win-win for everyone. It's not perfect, but it is a big improvement.

Here is the upside. If they didn't book you this time, they might book you next time. They will need a speaker next time and odds are they will not want to book the same speaker next time. If you were selected for the short list, since you were obviously high on the selection list this time (that's why they put the hold on your calendar) and unless you have made a pest of yourself, your chances will be better next time. Unless you plan to retire or die soon, this is a good thing. Be thankful for the holds that didn't close on your calendar when the date passed. They are seeds for future bookings!

This business is very time sensitive. Anything a speaker does to infringe upon that time element is going to cause agents to be unwilling to promote them in the future.

In the past, speakers would interrogate me or our agents when we would call to release a hold (and we thought we were doing the speaker a service by releasing it).

Why did the other speaker get picked and not me? I'm taller, I have better hair, I live closer, I have been speaking longer, I have nicer clothes, and I have sold more books than him or her. It's like high school, but with money! The 'stupid meter' starts going in the red, and it does not end well.

Look, I get it, feedback is the breakfast of champions, but most of the time we don't know if they chose the other speaker because they had a better video, a better program description, they were taller, or had more hair. (If it's the last two, I would definitely lose!)

Now, when I get interrogated, I have been known to say, "The president decided to hire his out of work brother-in-law so he can pay some bills. Hope it works out for them." That usually stops the stupid conversation.

Meeting planners rely on bureaus to supply speakers for meetings. More and more of this activity is taking place. Typically, a bureau will suggest three to six speakers for one slot on the program. This strategy, plus giving the meeting planner other options, is a good start.

It is better for your bureau rep or agent to be on the phone trying to sell you to a potential client then it is to be on the phone explaining to you why you didn't get a booking or a hold evaporated.

If a low percentage of your holds are turning into bookings, the problem is not the bureaus; it is quite probably your promotional material. It might be the copy; it might be the graphic design, your photo, or maybe the video is not inspiring people to hire you. Maybe your video is too old, and it is apparent by the content, hair, clothing styles, and needs updated. It might be a combination.

If you were sending your promotional material out to one hundred potential buyers and only a few, or worse nobody, booked you, what makes you think a bureau can do better?

At this point, aside from input from the bureau, the weight of the client's decision rests on the promotional material that you supplied to the bureau. Saving a few bucks on your promotional material and video production can cost you a fortune.

Also, spending a ton of money on amazing media kit that makes you look and sound better than you really are will come back and haunt you.

It makes me crazy and sad when speakers who should know better do not invest in materials that showcase what they offer in the best light.

When a speaker responds to our request for materials by saying something like, "The video I'm sending isn't my best work (or my best program or my signature speech or the best quality or it was shot in a church for a pro bono opportunity) or "the video is an hour long" or "I'm working on a new brochure, but it's not ready," I'm thinking...that is like showing up for a six-figure job interview dressed in a Hawaiian shirt and flip-flops like you are going to a Jimmy Buffet concert. What were you thinking?

This was the one I'll never forget. It was 1998, and we still had a big fancy office.

One of the junior agents who sorted the mail and checked in the 10 or 20 media kits we received daily from speakers looking for representation walks into my office and says: "Frank, you have got to see this. It's way too funny. It must be a mistake."

He inserts the VHS tape into the player, so I clicked 'Save' on the file I was working on, took a sip of coffee, leaned back in my chair, as the tape starts with an intro to a dating show for a cable station in Los Angeles. About 15 seconds into it, he hands me the media kit and I start to look at it while this singles dating show is playing. I confirm it really is her on the tape hosting the show, and this is her media kit.

This has to be a mistake. We are all human; we are not perfect, and her media kit has some positive things in it. Her kit claims she has years of experience as a trainer for one of the big seminar companies and she has pretty good energy. More agents and assistants come into my office until it is standing room only and together we watch this show, laughing and laughing at the clever and risqué repartee in the first round of questioning.

Well, I shut down this impromptu meeting at the commercial break because nobody was dialing for dollars, and we saw all we needed to see.

I kept her file on my desk and put it in my briefcase to take home to call her that evening. Sidebar here: I can call meeting and event planners during the day, and they will take the call, most of the time, from about 8 to 6, but I cannot call them in the evenings. I am willing and able to spend more time with a speaker on the phone during the non-prime time in the evenings.

So I call Lisa. She is from New York, she is Italian, she is a cool lady, and excited to get my call. She says, "I sent out over 100 media kits, and you are the only one who called me." She went on to say, "I swear, it is easier to get into the Mafia than it is to get into the speakers bureaus."

We both chuckled, and having seen my fair share of 'wise guy' movies, it was probably true. I said, "Well, might I ask you some questions?" She said sure. I asked if she knew she sent us the wrong tape. Now the conversation got very interesting.

She said it was the tape she intended because it was (in her mind) the best one she had of her being witty and interesting. Again, she is hosting a dating game show on the video, and she wants the agents at the bureau to market her for time management and stress management seminars. Really?

She says to me, "I thought they could see how I am on TV as a host for a dating show, and they can make the leap to know I would be good on stage."

I explained to her that there was a big disconnect here. This was like her wanting to buy a new Corvette and the dealer offering to let her test drive a used pick-up truck. Then, she informed me she is from Brooklyn and doesn't drive or even have a license.

Now I had an even bigger disconnect. So, I suggested if she walked into Mama Leone's Pizza and ordered a large, meat lovers pizza with extra cheese, but they brought out vegetarian lasagna, could she see the problem? She said, "No, I like vegetarian lasagna."

More disconnect.

So I said. "Let's imagine you were at a fashion show and you saw the perfect dress and shoes for you to go for a night out on the town, and the theater."

She said, "I love clothes and nice shoes, and the theater."

Now we're getting somewhere, I thought. So enthusiastically, I said, "OK, let's imagine you go shopping for the perfect dress like you saw at the fashion show, and the sales person keeps showing you ugly dresses that make you look bad and shoes that remind you of work boots."

I continued, "Our agents are like the salespeople in the store, they need the correct video to sell you."

And Lisa said: "Oh crap! I just wasted thousands of dollars on media kits and postage."

And I just said to myself: Too bad when things don't work out.

I knew a sharp guy. We traveled locally in the same circles for years. He wrote his first book, and I liked the book he wrote. I saw the potential in him. I had reasonable expectations that he was experienced, as he had been around the business world for many years. He was a cancer survivor.

He said he was a good speaker (of course everyone says that!) and I kept asking him for a five-minute demo video. He held me off for months, even called me up and said a group contacted him about speaking for them and asked if would I negotiate the deal and take care of the booking for him. I asked, "Why don't you do it?" And he said, "Well I would rather have you handle it. I don't like doing that stuff.

Out of friendship I said I'd do it for him. I had to slash our commission, and it turned out to be the lowest dollar booking in over 10 years.

We lost money on the deal, which caused raised eyebrows at our next board meeting.

Then the time comes for him to do the speech and he did not do well. His evaluations were below 50's; his PowerPoint failed, he started late, and he missed the mark. Now the client was justifiably angry, even though we were brought in to just write the contract after the client selected and agreed to book the speaker. But, because I put our company reputation on the line for this guy, we were slimed.

Then finally, he sent us two DVD's that were shot by amateurs with dreadful sound and lighting, expecting us to edit them for free. Oh well, live and learn.

Most bureaus are not in the video production business, but all bureaus are in the marketing business. Most bureaus (if they have been around for 10 years or more) can tell you what works and what doesn't work.

This is a touchy subject: Do you believe it is right and fair to ask an agent or bureau manager for their professional opinion? Is it right and fair to expect them to give you feedback, recommendations, and advice on how to improve your brand, media materials, and video to make more money, and do it for free? Time is money. Life is short. Real expertise is worth something. How much is it worth to you to learn how to make millions of dollars? Think about it.

Summary: This is a great secret: Be easy to work with. Pay attention to the details. Focus on your marketing and bureau relationships. Make everything you do matter.

CHAPTER 10

Make It Easy For the Agent, Bureau, Client, and Yourself

In 2004, our bureau booked me for a group-training seminar combining the topics of leadership and customer service. Since this was going to be packed with interactive content, and they demanded a lot of customization, I created a 12-page handout along with references and links to web pages I built for them to download books, tools, white pages, and software trials. Plus, they approved some affiliate links that were back-end profit options.

They did, however, insist and put in the contract that the handout would have to be sent for approval at least three weeks in advance. That was fine because I like to have my outline, media show, and handout done one month before a show.

They also insisted on making copies of the handout that they would have ready to distribute at the event.

I must admit, I am not comfortable with people doing this because I have had people do an awful print job on the handout. This reflects badly on me, as it would on any speaker.

Against my better judgment, I took a leap of faith and figured I would be there in plenty of time to fix any problems; plus, it was one less thing I had to pack and carry on the plane.

Well, you know the old cliché, if anything can go wrong, it will. The flight was cancelled. I had to take a backup flight. It was after midnight when I arrived at the hotel. The sound check was for 7 am.

The show started at 8 am; I went on from 9 to noon. After the sound check, I asked the event planner for the handouts. She gave me a blank stare and admitted in all the hustle and bustle of the event she forgot them.

I smiled and said, don't worry; I'll take care of it. I happened to notice a copy shop on the same block as the hotel, so I grabbed my master file with the original of the handout, and my credit card, and hurried down there.

Fortunately, there were three employees who just finished a big job and the machines were available. I explained my predicament; they jumped right on it, and they all received an extra 20-dollar tip from me for the extra fast service and attention to detail. I was back at 8:20 and we were golden. The handouts looked great; the show went great, and we booked several spin-off dates with other speakers and trainers. It's nice when things work out.

There is more to the story: The client had shared some stories with me how they were burned by other speakers in the past on the expenses and the cost of handouts. They made it clear to me that they watch every penny.

Now, I could have billed them for the cost of the handouts, and been justified in doing it. I could have made a stand, pulled out the contract they signed, and pointed to the additional handout clause they had to have in the contract. I even had printed the emails correspondence confirming they received and approved the final handout, and it was going to be printed.

It was a matter of less than a hundred bucks, and it would have caused problems for the planner and her getting called out by her bosses for this. I considered it an opportunity to build the relationship. I said nothing and I ate the cost out of my pocket. It was a small price to pay for a long-term relationship.

Best practice: Don't be a problem, be the solution.

A couple years ago we booked several speakers for one event on the east coast. A couple of them are on our "A" List of favorites, and the other two were speakers the client wanted us to book for them. One of them was a humorist who thought it was funny to call the meeting planner and the bureau the night before the event and leave a voicemail telling us he was delayed someplace west of Idaho and would not make the event on the east coast. At least, *he* thought this was being funny.

I heard the beginning of his message; I started hyperventilating, I got chest pains and dropped the cell phone. The worst part was I was just less than 10 minutes away from going on stage at a church for a pro-bono course I was teaching for Dave Ramsey called Financial Peace University.

I collapsed in a chair, my dear friends saw me and rushed to my aid. I caught my breath and told them what happened. They panicked, but I said, "Let me call the speaker."

Well, he answered his cell phone and said, "Oh, ha ha, I was just kidding; I was playing a practical joke on you and the client and you both fell for it."

Not a big "HA HA".

BIG MISTAKE.

When I found out what he done it to our client as well, I got chest pains again. I was livid. In all the years I have been in business and involved in booking thousands of events, I never had anyone do anything this stupid. It was improper, unprofessional, inappropriate, immature, and deplorable.

We lost the client over it. The speaker's reputation is permanently damaged, and it will cost him hundreds of thousands of dollars in bookings. It also guaranteed he would never see another booking from us.

"Forgive your enemies, but never forget their names." – **John F. Kennedy**

Best practice: This is a serious business. Don't be a problem; be a joy to work with.

Again it is worth noting here, things happen and most of the time things go smoothly. Time to time people do stupid things. Stuff happens; nobody is perfect. The stories of the mistakes are good lessons for us to learn from, I hope you will agree.

Speakers who work to make the process of marketing, booking, and delivering speeches easy for both the bureau and the bureau's clients get recommended by bureaus much more than speakers who do not. Speakers who have good marketing materials are more likely to get hired by meeting planners.

Supplying the bureau with good promotional material helps them book you.

There are two sides to every story. Here is the tale of one event.

One speaker did an excellent job on the platform. The audience loved her. She earned rave reviews from the meeting planner.

The evaluation turned into the bureau by the speaker displayed all excellent scores.

However, over the telephone, the meeting planner reported a different story. She said the speaker was difficult to work with, made too many demands, and did not do her homework to learn about the group and missed the mark. The speaker had showed up on site demanding AV needs she had never told them about beforehand and that were not in the contract or in the budget.

The meeting planner went on to explain this was not mentioned on the evaluation because she did not want her boss to be aware of the problems. In this case, the speaker will never know about her bad report because the meeting planner asked the bureau not to mention it to her, and the bureau is beholding to the meeting planner, not the speaker. The incident will forever cast a shadow on the bureau's opinion of the speaker, the situation has damaged her reputation, and it will likely cost her much opportunity in the future.

Being easy to work with does not mean you have to sell your soul, compromise your principles, or do anything you do not want to do. It does mean you should understand who is serving whom, and be reasonably flexible.

"Many speakers don't realize how difficult their offices may be to work with, and we cannot afford the extra hassle and time to deal with such staff. We go elsewhere."

Andrea Gold

Gold Stars Speakers Bureau

A small town business owner once said, "The only job description I have is to satisfy my customers." This philosophy is one that recognizes "it's all about them."

Anticipating customer wants and needs, and making it easy for them to do business with you, is a winning strategy.

Be A Partner

Arrive early and stay late at events. Promote the bureau when on site at the event.

Do a great job so there will be opportunities for spin-off business, and be diligent about tracking where your business comes from so that you can refer them back to the bureau that the lead came from.

Those who partner with others in business, look for partners who produce. Profit is the tape measure of the free market. Profit is what you have left over after you pay everybody. Many in the speaking profession do not understand this.

Wise speakers like to partner with bureaus that assist them to earn profits by bringing them paid bookings. Likewise, bureaus like to partner with speakers who help them earn profits by bringing leads back from the speaking engagements.

Speakers booked the most are those who are easy to work with and report back following their speaking engagements. Open communication regarding leads and spin-offs is crucial to maintaining a good relationship with a bureau.

Speaking is not selling. You could do a good job on the platform for some people you cannot reach in a sales capacity. A bureau partner can get additional business for you by selling your speaking services to people who will not buy from you.

A bureau benefits both the client and the speaker. The convenience for the client is making only one call and one description of what they are seeking.

The speaker, trainer, or entertainer benefits by saving time and vast expenses when a reputable bureau suggests their presentations or shows them to hundreds of established clients.

As a matter of choice, many meeting planners do not want to deal with the speaker on business matters. They don't want to offend a speaker with offers they think may not be appropriate. They do not want to have to rely on you to shoot straight about your capabilities. They don't want to have to tell you "no" if they decide to go in some other direction. They don't want the speaker to pester them with sales persistence. They would rather deal with an agent or a partner in a bureau, as a buffer to go between them and the speaker.

When the speaker brings back leads for future business it not only tells me that the speaker did a great job, but also that this speaker is acting as my on-site business partner.

Giving a great speech is a minimum requirement. Being easy to work with is a plus.

Delivering business opportunities back to the bureau is what gets you on the "A Team."

To have a good long-term business relationship with a bureau you have to produce leads that lead to bookings.

Great evaluations are nice. They confirm your work was more than adequate in meeting the minimum standard. As a professional speaker you are expected to be good. That's why the meeting planner is willing to pay your fee.

The bureau agent, who booked you, expects you to be good enough to produce spin-offs. If you never do, they will begin to question either your talent or your integrity.

When you become known as a speaker who delivers spin-offs and repeat engagements, one who is in the business to do business, your bureau business will grow. Like you, bureaus are eager to partner with those who produce.

"Wait a minute," some speakers protest, "Those spin-offs came about because of me!"

If that is your attitude, your outlook for building profitable business relationships with speakers' bureaus is not bright. If your service is in such demand that you do not need people who speak highly of you, vouch for you, recommend you to their clients, and produce business for you, perhaps you do not need to work with agents at bureaus.

However, if you do want to tap into the hundred thousand speaking engagements booked by bureaus each year, you've got to be a team player. When you get a lead as a result of a spin-off, send it to the bureau and let them handle it.

Working it yourself, keeping the bureau posted, and sending them a commission if the date books is not how to become known as a good partner. It is a good way to prevent future bureau business.

It Takes Just a Few Things to Build a Winning Team

You can only have a winning team when you commit to leading a team of people who **WANT** to be winners. Ask any winning coach how they did it. They will tell you they had good leadership, teamwork, a good plan, and the inspiration to execute the plan to the best of their ability.

Everyone has to care about doing things well. So chose to partner with bureaus that are excited about the business and WANT to do things right.

Success does not come by accident; it comes on purpose. Team up with those who plan ahead, and have a plan for everything.

Always play as a team. You want to hitch your wagon to those who understand working together increases the odds for success and will honor commitments to execute the plans together.

Be About Developing Future Bureau Relationships

All current business relationships are subject to change, for many reasons. Your relationship with an agent or bureau can change for any of the following reasons:

- You reached saturation with their client base. Most bureaus have "X" number of regular clients. It is possible to run through the potential a bureau has to offer you. It's not the end of the game, but the flow of business will slow down.
- Your fees have increased and less of their clients can afford you.
- You bomb.
- The bureau sells out or goes under.
- Bureaus merge and the new enterprise is moving in a new direction.
- People retire and people die.

Take advantage of all of the opportunities you have to develop relationships with additional bureaus.

Opportunity is knocking when any of the following is taking place:

- A bureau's client asks for or about you.
- The bureau hears good things about you from another speaker they trust.
- The bureau hears about you from another bureau.
- Someone from the bureau hears you speak. (Be sure to invite them when you are speaking nearby.)
- The bureau starts losing dates to you.
- A last minute emergency when a bureau needs you to cover a date nearby.
- You have developed a good program with a new twist on a marketable topic.

These scenarios cover most of the ways speaker-bureau relationships originate. When any of these opportunities sprouts for you, be sure to cultivate them. (Notice that calling a bureau on the phone and saying, "you ought to book me" is not on the list.)

Cultivating business relationships is about teamwork. Each party has to contribute some things, and be willing to give up other things for the good of the group. This collaboration leads to opportunity to share in a more abundant harvest.

If you focus only on what you have to give up, bureaus will not be a good fit for you.

On the other hand, if you can see that your time and talent is more valuable when it is devoted to programs and presentations while someone else handles sales, marketing, booking, billings, etc., you will recognize the advantages that accrue to those who work with good agents and bureaus.

Even if you hire people to do all these other things, you've got to pay to get it done. When you pay bureau commissions, you do not have to provide them with vacations, insurance benefits, and all of the other baggage and drama that comes with in-house employees.

To survive, your speaking business must be profitable. The true measure, then, is not the number of dates, the number of standing ovations, and certainly not the number of people you have on your staff or team. The true measure is what you have left over after everybody (including Uncle Sam) is paid.

When you save a dollar or two on travel, pass it on to the client. When you pick up a lead while doing a bureau date, pass it on to the bureau.

Be a valuable asset to agents, bureaus and their clients.

Don't overcharge anyone for anything. I could easily write a long and entertaining chapter on the crazy and radical things I have seen on expense reports. Some of these speakers and entertainers are not around anymore, but I can just sum it up by saying they were complex walking monuments to very bad behavior.

You want to be known in the marketplace as a value, even if your fee is impressive. The fair market price of all valuable goods and services is determined by supply and demand. If you are working too much, your price is too low. If you are not working as much as you would like to work, it's possible the opposite is true. It's also possible there are flaws in your marketing and media packages.

A good speaker is willing to give more to the client than the client expects. They go the extra mile to keep expenses low for the client.

Meeting planners are held accountable when a conference runs over budget.

Unexpected expenses by speakers or entertainers cause them to protest to the agents and bureau. This causes trouble, problems, and embarrassment for your premium level customers.

Plus, when clients call the bureau to complain, it takes up the bureau's time and flattens their spirit and momentum. It's better to have bureaus promoting you than defending you.

It is better for clients to be greeted with pleasant surprises.

Being fair and honest is really simple. How do you expect to be treated by those who supply the things you want and need? How do you expect to be treated by your partners?

"Do Unto Others, As You Would Have Them Do Unto You."
Matthew 7:12

The golden rule is very sound business strategy. It is essential for maintaining business relationships.

If you accept a hold from a bureau, honor the hold. If you accept a date from a bureau, play by the bureau's rules and send them the spin-offs.

When various parties enter into agreements that require the exchange of money, those who are spending the money expect those who are receiving it to be credible, and to exercise good business ethics. If the buyers are ever disappointed, the arrangement and subsequent agreements will cease.

Some people come into the speaking and entertainment profession from various backgrounds where they have not had the opportunity to learn about acceptable business behavior and business ethics. There are some things that are legal and moral, but not ethical in business circles.

There is a simple test for business ethics: *If it will cause reasonable and legitimate clients to sever their business relationship with you, it is not ethical.* It's not very smart either. It is very hard to grow a profession or a business when you often lose clients because of unwise or unethical behavior.

Do Not Fluctuate With Your Fee

Somewhere between the staunch fee, and the free stance (on one extreme) and the 'whatever the traffic will bear' approach on the other, there has to be a flexible high ground of fee credibility.

Obviously, no sales professionals are going to back their futures on selling a specific service that can be bought somewhere else for less. At the same time, there are circumstances where business prudence dictates some degree of negotiable flexibility.

In the interest of maintaining both credibility and flexibility, these are some suggested approaches:

Publish your fee schedule and keep it simple. Example: Events within the U.S. for up to one hour you charge $X,000.00. For international events outside of the U.S. you charge $Y,000,00. It's simple.

A presenter sent us a fee schedule that stated he was based near the Ohio and PA border. His fee for anything in the eastern time zone was his lowest fee, say $X, then he stated anything in the Central Standard time Zone was 50% more, say $Y, and anything in the Pacific Time Zone was 100% more than $X, so let's call that $Z.

Now I asked him, how long does it take to fly to fly from Pittsburg to Miami, Florida? He said, it's about two and a half to three hour flight. Then I asked how long does it take to fly to Chicago? He said, less than two hours. So I asked, then why does it cost more for Chicago than Miami? That's not simple.

Now here is a caveat: If you want to work locally, you might want to offer a local fee, but make sure your agent knows about it.

Publish any discounts offered.

Be diligent to keep bureaus in the loop about any new discounts offered or other acceptable variances.

Never undercut anyone who is trying to sell your services.

When it makes good business sense to be flexible, then negotiate travel, terms, product sales, and other items rather than the fee.

Good business relationships are built on integrity, and good bureaus work hard to protect their reputations with their clients.

Both speakers and bureaus have a responsibility to deal honestly and fairly with clients.

Final words on honesty: Do not do business with people you do not trust. Do not expect people to do business with you if you are not worthy of their trust. Working with a speakers' bureau is a business relationship.

Be Smart

There are some reputable bureaus that just may not be a good fit for you and your business style. You should ask up front about a bureau's policies and procedures on important issues of interest to you.

Knowing the things you need to know, before a relationship begins, will save you headaches and heartaches.

There will be times when reputable bureaus that are a good fit for you present you with certain offers or opportunities. These offers may or may not make sense for you at the time. Do not hesitate to say NO when a project is not in the best interest of your business.

You should always have sound reasons for all of the business decisions you make. When it comes to your money, you get to call the shots.

Other opportunities you may be offered from bureaus include things such as special sections on the bureau's website or special inclusion in a brochure or mail out. Some, from time to time, offer campaigns. Again, weigh the opportunity in terms of your best interests to make sure it is indeed an opportunity for you and not just a good deal for them.

Due to the nature of business, sometimes it is smart to do things that on the surface appear to be dumb. I have given direct dates to bureaus, giving up the commission. That may appear to be dumb, but it was smart in the long run. They dealt with a client that would have taken up a bunch of my time and resources, and that bureau had a relationship with the client and geographically was closer to them. It helped me develop relationships that led to much more business.

Go Early & Stay Late

Smart speakers go early and stay late. They work the crowd while they are on site, even when they are not on the platform. They know people like to do business with people they know, and they like to hire speakers who have been attentive to them.

Make friends before your presentation, and you will have cheerleaders in the crowd when you go on, even before you deliver your opening line. Staying late will provide an opportunity for those who were impressed with your presentation to ask for information. They can't hire you if you are not there.

Big tip here: Make friends and play nice with the audio-visual team working the event. These people meet and watch many speakers and work with many different meeting planners throughout the years.

Back in Jr. High School, I was in the A-V club. We would deliver the overhead projectors and slide projectors to teacher's classrooms and set them up. Here it is 50 years later and the technology has advanced significantly, but the concept of amplifying sound and plugging in a projector to show an image on a screen is still the same.

The A/V folks are your friends and your lifeline in the rooms. Countless times I have asked the audience to acknowledge the hardworking meeting planners and A-V Crew, knowing that while I might be up on stage all alone, pouring my heart out, there is a whole crew of people working the show, adjusting the lights and sound, making it a magnificent experience for the audience, and rarely are these hard-working people appreciated for making the speaker or entertainer look good.

I always carry extra cash to pass out to the really good ones for a job well done. These tokens of my appreciation, along with the hand-written thank you notes I write while waiting to board airplanes and in taxis, these kind gestures have paid me back in great referrals over the years. What goes around comes around.

Spin-offs will increase if you go to the receptions, hang around the platform after the program, and work the exhibit hall. If it's a bureau date, send the leads to the bureau. Be smart and work smart.

Rapid Response Pays Off
When you get a call from a bureau, respond quickly. We live in a real-time customer engagement world.
When a meeting planner gets ready to book a speaker, they are anxious to get it done and move on to other things. When a bureau is in the final stages of negotiations and is trying to close a sale, they are anxious to get it done. Sales can be missed because of delays. Be smart and respond quickly before you lose the momentum and the opportunity dissipates.

Gifts to Bureaus
You might buy marginal business, but it is much more profitable to earn good business. Tokens of appreciation for business already done are much more respectable.

Do's and don'ts for speakers who play it smart:

- Do not recommend your friends to bureaus unless you know the bureau will be glad you did.
- Do keep the bureau in the loop as you deal with their clients, and report to them shortly after the presentation. I advise doing it the same day. I have programmed myself to contact the agent at the bureau who booked the date as soon as I get back to the hotel room or into the taxi on the way to the airport. My calls are always to the point and factual. Here is how they go.

Ring, ring: Thank you for calling the speakers bureau, how may I help you?

Hello, this is Frank, is Joyce available for a two-minute update on the event we just finished? (Over 90% of the time I get through.)

Joyce: Hey Frank, how did it go?

Frank: Thanks for taking my call Joyce. Is this a good time to talk for two minutes?

Joyce: Yes sure, please tell me how was the event?

Frank: The event went very well. Your clients, Mike and Renee, are very happy. I believe the evaluations from the audience, based on their reactions, will be good to excellent. You can discuss that with Renee and let me know.

The A-V team had an issue with the sound system after my sound check and before I went on for my presentation. Someone kicked a wire on the wall, we found the problem and fixed it before it was an issue.

Mike wants to speak with you about a booking for a group in the spring on the subject of aviation safety. I suggested he speak with you about this and one other opportunity for a board retreat soon. He needs a facilitator for the first meeting to do a teambuilding experience for them.

I expect to be traveling until late in the evening, so I will return to my office in the morning and send over my expense report by 9 am. Also look for three business cards from audience members that inquired about booking me for events in Colorado, New Mexico, and California. I'll include all the details.

Do you have any other questions for me?

Joyce, who is panting and giddy with joy at this point says, "OMG, you are awesome, I love you!"

Frank: "Love you too, thanks for the opportunity. Talk to you soon. Bye-bye."

Joyce: "Bye." Click.

One other strategy I have used is photographing each prospects business card with my smart phone, and include my notes on their event, and email or text it to the agent so they can get on it fast. They love this.

Moving forward

- Do not sell products without prior approval from the bureau, and when you have approval, be smart and do not oversell.
- Do include your bureau partner in on the profits of product sales. That is part of the deal.
- Do submit travel expenses as soon as possible after the date, preferably within twenty-four hours. I usually do mine on the plane, or in the car on the way back from the event. That way when I hit the office, I can send it off to the agent fast, and cross that off my list.

- Do not get into a confrontation with a bureau over procedures. They are your customers, so do it their way.
- Do not expect a bureau to hold your hand and get you to the event. Get a map, use a GPS, call the hotel to confirm your reservation, and plan your entire trip ahead of time. While I have people in my office who do this daily, I still double-check every detail. It takes less than 20 minutes, and I have total peace of mind.

Quick story: We received a call from an egomaniacal entertainer who flew into New Orleans for an event we booked for him. From his limo, he called his assistant in California and told her to call us in Florida to tell us he was in the limo, he was lost, and wanted us to call the hotel and get him directions to the hotel. The hotel was three blocks away.

It was a Saturday and my turn on the after-hours phone. I said, "OK, no problem, stay on the line, I'll take care of it right now. Put me through to the limo driver." Problem solved. Smart phones are amazing! But, his likeability score just took a hit.

Back to reality.

- Do attend the meal functions where you are speaking, and eat with the group.
- Do send master copies of handouts and anything else you plan to leave behind, to the bureau well in advance.
- Do not recommend speakers to the agents' or bureau's clients. That's the bureau's job. You can and should discuss opportunities, events, dates, and topics, but not specific speakers or fees.
- Do tell the truth, the whole truth, and nothing but the truth to bureaus and their clients.
- Do not use offensive material in your presentations, especially when working for a bureau's client. It's a difficult mess the agents and clients will have to clean up later.

- Do be the kind of partner you would want as your partner.
- Do not book a spin-off directly. Refer it to the bureau. We may work in a national market, but this is a cozy industry, and they will find out.
- Do not pester agents or bureaus with frequent keeping in touch phone calls.
- Do have a unique topic or a different twist or spin on a common topic.
- Do return phone calls to bureaus quickly, preferably within a couple of hours and on the same day. (Chances are the client is looking for a speaker and you are not the only one.)
- Do not discuss fees with the bureau's client. It may seem appropriate to you, but it will not seem appropriate to the bureau and the bureau is your customer.
- Do go out of your way to satisfy both the bureau and their client before the date, as well as when on site.
- Do make sure your A-V needs and all other specific or unusual needs, are made known to the client well in advance. I prefer to include them in a contract rider or addendum.
- Do not bother the bureau's clients with your problems: travel, accommodations, or otherwise. Call the bureau if you have issues.
- Do not tell the bureau's clients how they should run their meetings.
- Do not criticize the bureau or bureaus in general when with the client. Again, this is a cozy industry. What you say will get back to them.
- Do not expect a bureau to make your career a success. That's up to you.
- Do not expect a bureau to design your promotional material.
- Do supply the bureau with the proper tools to sell your services.
- Do your homework so you will be able to do a great job for the agent and bureau's client.

- Do not give a speech that was not what the client expected, and do not mess up the client's program by cutting your presentation short or running over your time.
- Do not expect a bureau to review or keep any unsolicited material you send.
- Do express your appreciation to the bureau for the dates you get, and do not complain about the ones you don't get.
- Do discuss any problems with the bureau; they need to know as soon as possible.
- Do not show up late for an engagement.
- Do ask permission, through the bureau, before you take anyone with you to the date.
- Do keep the bureau in the loop on a timely basis should you incur unexpected travel problems so they can be in the process of arranging a backup.

Absolute No No's:

(This is a compilation of replies from numerous bureaus when asked why they have terminated relationships with speakers.)

- Never be dishonest with the bureau or the client.
- Never undercut the price quoted by the bureau.
- Never be difficult to work with, either with the bureau or the bureau's client.
- Never do anything on or off the platform that upsets the bureau's client.
- Never give out your phone number, website, or any other contact information while doing a bureau date. If you are asked for contact information, give them the name of your agent and the bureau's phone number.
- Never direct book a spin-off or repeat engagement that belongs to a bureau.

There will be times when two or more bureaus bump into one another chasing a client like ballplayers chasing a fly ball. You may get caught in the middle.

Take comfort in knowing it is not your place to protect bureaus from one another. The free market will solve the problem. Customers decide which speaker to hire and which bureau will get to book the job.

When bureaus are competing for business, your only obligation is to deal with each in an evenhanded manner, honor any holds giving bureaus time to talk with their clients and stay out of the process. The deal goes to the one who gets the order. May the best team win!

Invest Wisely in Your Material & Your Presentation

As was said in the beginning, the best way to market a speaking career through bureaus or other options is to do a very good job on the platform. The greater portion of future opportunity comes about because of those who have been impressed by your presentations in the past.

Do the best job you can do every time you present; work hard to gain as much recognition in the industry as you can, and be nice to people. Always be nice to people. This is the time tested, play it smart strategy that has worked for most of today's top speakers.

I am quite amazed at the talent among speakers, from knowledge to platform skills and sense of humor. The ones who gain my greatest respect are the ones with these elements, who are very humble and caring, on top of their obvious talent."

Andrea Gold

Gold Stars Speakers Bureau

Remember, the goal of business is to make money, but doing business is not about money. It's always about people. People decide what to buy, when to buy, where to buy, how much to buy, and people decide which speakers to hire and which speakers to bring back.

Smart speakers are both good and nice. You have to be both to get spin-offs and repeats, the bread and butter of the speaking profession.

In Summary: Do good work. Be fair and honest. Make it easy for your customer to do business with you. This is not difficult and will get you known in a way that will help your business flourish.

Free market buyers seek value, and value is the work product of service. Make it your business to serve those who want and need your service.

I hope that what you have read so far is of benefit to you. The information and ideas you have found in this book are based on what has worked for me for over 40 years. It has been my intention to simply share ideas and information. Thank you for reading so far. Keep going, the best is yet to come.

CHAPTER 11

Trend Towards "Managed Speakers" Options

Here is how managed speaker option works: An established speaker will enter into an agreement with an agent to allow them to represent the speaker or talent in the marketplace.

This agent will keep their marketing content and videos updated with speakers bureaus. In addition they will assist with the speakers with most or all of their bookings with clients and in most cases the speakers bureaus without a commission split, (unlike the normal co-broker arrangement) and for this the agent will receive a monthly fee from the speaker.

Contrary to what some believe, this is not a new trend. Speakers, authors, entertainers, and sports figures have used the services of exclusive, professional managers for well over 50 years.

However, over the last decade more popular and prominent speakers and authors have chosen to go with a speaker management arrangement for bookings, managed sponsorship opportunities and book promotional tours. This allows them to simplify their lives, and in some cases, reduce or eliminate their in-house marketing, and support team.

In most cases, this allows for speakers to have professional representation and provides for the agents at speakers bureaus to work with competent professionals who can get things done with efficiency. Or at least that is how it is supposed to work in theory.

These relationships can do very well for years, or crash in a short time, or slowly disintegrate over months or years. I've seen it all.

A few important issues our research and conversations with agents has made glaringly obvious is that the spin-off business going back to the agent or bureaus, is more than with managed speakers, by over 50% in a majority of cases.

One can surmise the independent speaker had not developed a good system to track, explore and confirm referrals from spin-off business.

Another issue in the marketplace is when speakers who deliver customized presentations should be available for conference calls with potential clients.

This can get complicated with an extra layer of representation, and sometimes make it more difficult and time-consuming to get the needed information and things done.

Some speakers who enter into an exclusive agreement with an agent who splits commissions have noticed a significant drop-off in business in their bureau business. For some it is a greed factor that I believe does not serve the client in the best way.

If a client calls ABC Bureau looking for a particular speaker, and that speaker who previously was listed with ABC Bureau has now gone exclusive with XYZ Bureau, in most cases, both must agree to accept a commission split, and make about half of what they used to make.

Sometimes it works well and sometimes it doesn't. You are going to have to figure out what is going to work well for you.

One solution I came up with for the two bureaus that represent me in a co-broker deal is to offer them more commission so everybody is happier. A high percentage of those situations turn out well. I am grateful for the work and thankful they are recommending of me.

Summary: This managed speaker option is not for everybody. It works better for established speakers who have more inquiries for speaking opportunities than they can handle, and for people who can afford a professional manager.

Is it for you? The answer lies within you.

CHAPTER 12

The Real Rocket Man

There are specific characteristics every agent looks for in talent.

Authenticity is a very big one. The authentic speaker is a person who has truly been there and done it. A person who has led the team to victory, overcome what for most would be unbelievable and impossible odds, and he or she did it with integrity, character, confidence, courage, and humility.

For over a decade, it has been my honor and privilege to represent and share the stage with a truly authentic American Icon, Author, Top Gun Pilot, Astronaut, Space Shuttle Commander, and speaker with the "Right Stuff", Rick Searfoss.

On many occasions I have stated, "If I could find several more speakers with the characteristics, accomplishments, work ethic, and commitment to excellence that Rick exemplifies every day, I could ride their accomplishments like a horse into the sunset for the rest of my career."

First, Rick believes in his creator, and I know he has a deep faith that guides his life.

Back in the spring of '06 when my dear mother passed away, I was on a two-day road trip driving from Florida to Ohio for the funeral. On the morning of the second day, I was driving on Route 75 just north of Knoxville, Tennessee and in a moment of great sadness, loss, and despair it hit me hard: she was really gone.

I was pounding on the dashboard and questioning my creator, when in a flash of divine order or divine intervention, Rick happened to call and talked with me for over an hour. He put it all in perspective for the rest of the trip, and the rest of my life has been pretty darn good. Rick is not only a great speaker, he is a great and true friend.

He knows the importance of family and friends. Not only is he concerned with the legacy he will leave, but he also honors the legacy he has received and the traditions of his ancestors who came to America in the late 1700's.

Over the years, I have come to know his wonderful family. I have even had the opportunity to hold his first grandson on my lap. Just before I went to print with this book his daughter gave birth to their 3rd grandson.

Rick has a desire to advance culture. When he leaves the world, it will be a better place.

He has a powerful and realistic vision to lead. With long-term thinking, Rick leads with the realization his actions today will affect his life and others in the future.

Rick has gratitude. He works hard and is thankful for everything he receives.

Rick improves his physical health. He knows his body is a sanctuary. He works to improve his health and his image. Rick is in great shape, he exercises daily and eats properly, and he still fits in his flight suit from over 35 years ago. I wish I could say that, and I bet most of you do too!

Rick is confident. This doesn't mean cocky by any means. In this business, it's not easy to keep your ego in check, yet Rick has consistently demonstrated to us he is the real deal with the right stuff. Our clients go out of their way to share with us what a nice, kind, and humble person he is. All of our agents and partners really like him too. He is the benchmark for "the best speaker ever" and how to do it all right.

He's committed and faithful. Rick says what he means and means what he says.

He follows through with his word even with people who don't follow through with their own. He is loyal in all of his relationships.

One afternoon I was opening mail and there was an envelope with a check for $4,250 from Rick Searfoss. There was a note letting us know that is was for a commission from a spin-off that he discovered had come about from an endeavor at the Atlantis Resort in the Bahamas.

Very few people have that kind of integrity and commitment to a relationship.

First, he had to do some inquiry with the client that most speakers and entertainers do not do. Once he determined the original source of the referral was our speakers bureau; Rick put a check in the mail the day he arrived home.

I was so grateful; I called to thank him and told him I was going to put the money into a specific marketing budget to promote him. That money generated many bookings for us. It's really nice when things work out.

Rick is always learning. He is coachable. He loves life and seeks to make the most out of it. Rick is always reading good books, and our regular discussions include what we are reading and learning.

Over the years, I have been in the audience for over 30 of his presentations around the world. Each time after his presentation, he looks me in the eye and asks for feedback. Rick knows feedback is the breakfast of champions.

And I give it to him, unfiltered and direct. No candy-coating anything with this guy.

Rick listens and isn't eager to hear the sound of his own voice. He doesn't interrupt and he follows the rule that more than 75% of the time should be listening vs. talking.

I know Rick takes my suggestions and recommendations to heart because his presentations keep getting better. Virtually every time he gets standing ovations and spin-off opportunities from our clients. Still, he is committed to working on improving and being the best, on and off stage.

By the way, it is worth noting here that Rick was chosen to be on a Wheaties Box for the Breakfast of Champions collector series. That's pretty cool!

He was also chosen the 2006, 2009 and 2012 Speaker of The Year Award winner! That is even cooler! He earned it.

Here is one of the secrets to success I hope you use and process from this book. Rick is successful because he made a commitment to developing his skills on stage. He has developed his own unique brand and marketing approach. He maintains great relationships with agents and clients. He makes customized presentations and exceeds the audiences and agents expectations. That's a multi-million dollar success tip.

Summary: Be the best you can be. Leave your ego at home. Focus on building your brand. Develop and work your marketing plan, presentation, and promotional material.

CHAPTER 13

Trust the Voice of Experience
What I learned from Frank Sinatra

When I was a young man, I had the opportunity to meet some great people who had a huge impact on me.

One of them was Frank Sinatra. I met him in 1962 when I was 11 years old. We were backstage at The Front Row Theater in Cleveland, Ohio. My parents were invited to a meet and greet after his performance and I was the only kid in a Green Room full of adults. Mr. Sinatra saw me sitting alone on the couch; he walked over to me and said: "Hello, do you know who I am?"

I said, "I sure do, you're Mr. Frank Sinatra and my parents and I really enjoyed your show. Can I ask you a couple questions?"

Mr. Sinatra smiled, sat on the couch, and said, "What's your name?"

I said, "Frank, just like yours" and I smiled a big smile and he laughed. So, I started with this, "What was your favorite song from the show tonight?"

He quickly said, "All of them."

Then I asked, "What advice would give young people who want to be successful?"

Mr. Sinatra said, "People often remark that I'm pretty lucky. Luck is only important in so far as getting the chance to sell you at the right moment. After that, you've got to have talent and know how to use it."

I grinned and said, "Anything else?"

Mr. Sinatra gave me a few more jewels. "Take good care of your health and your body. Do something adventurous, stand up for yourself, and walk with a confident swagger."

One more time I asked: "Anything else?

He said; "Stay alive, stay active, and get as much practice as you can."

Ol' Blue Eyes lived by this mantra, and his reputation as a legendary singer and iconic player holds much truth in this statement. We can all take a cue from Frank Sinatra, so follow these bits of advice, and you'll be well on your way to becoming a classic yourself.

"You've got to be on the ball from the minute you step out into that spotlight. You gotta know exactly what you're doing every second on that stage; otherwise the act goes right into the bathroom. It's all over. Good night."

Frank Sinatra, Larry King Live, May 13, 1988

I learned later that Mr. Sinatra really enjoyed singing, *The Best Is Yet To Come*, and it is engraved on his tombstone.

Summary: What's your plan?

Who do you know that can advise you or assist you to go further?

What questions will you ask them?

CHAPTER 14

Publish or Perish
The Brave New World of Publishing

The good news is you have options. The bad news is you have competition.

However, in many cases the speaker or trainer that gets booked over the selection of speakers the clients are considering are the ones who are published on the subject they are expecting to have addressed in the keynote speech.

The same is true with songwriters. The ones who specialize in country get hired to write country songs; the same applies to rock and roll and the classics.

It's also true of screenwriters. The ones with the experience make it to the top of the list.

Anything Dan Poynter wrote about self-publishing is very good, and Rik Feeney's book "Writing Books for Fun, Fame & Fortune" is good too. See the website for links. www.publicspeakingformoney. com/books.

And be sure to read every word of Chapter 3 in, "Publish your Book or Reports or Else."

At this point, I am going to recommend you purchase and read and reread the book:

"How To Position Yourself As The Obvious Expert," by Elsom Eldridge, Jr., Mark L. Eldridge. www.publicspeakingformoney.com/books.

In my career, I had a few things that went in my favor. The one thing that worked for me was a lust for adventure and excitement, and I recorded them on film. The photos of my trips to exotic and wonderful places for adventure were in demand for magazines. But writing about them was not easy for me. Fortunately, I am a quick learner and a good note taker. I found good editors. I found people who were willing to publish them, along with my photographs. That's how it started for me.

Another adventure was making businesses work better or turning around failing enterprises. Also, inspiring groups of people to be better leaders and team members, raise the bar, look inside themselves, and look around outside of themselves for solutions and to discover the possibilities of improvement and engagement.

Those experiences always made for good stories and passive income.

Writers make a decent living by creating all kinds of stuff, like fiction and non-fiction books, songs, advertising, promotional copy, writing speeches, white papers, business plans, copy for websites, posts for blogs, Facebook, LinkedIn, Twitter, content courses, email marketing, and even greeting cards.

Back in the 1990's, I was the keynote speaker for a self-publishing conference in the South. While I was listing the many ways a writer could make a living, one of the audience members asked me, "What kind of writing pays best?"

I repeated the question, so everyone could hear it and process it; then I took a long dramatic pause, smiled and said: "Ransom notes!" The audience erupted in laughter.

The honest fact was I was attempting to buy a long moment to think of a better answer, and I wasn't too far off. Back then, believe it or not, the best legitimate pay-per-word was greeting cards.

There are several factors in writing. The first one is making sure you are good enough at it. Second, make sure it has enough rich and unique content so it will have appeal to many people. Third, choose a path of profit in publishing.

Big tip here: You can hire ghostwriters, editors, people who specialize in book layout, cover design, and publishing consultants. So you can get a book done by pros, and many people choose this path. Remember, it is your choice. The answer lies within you.

Over the years, I have watched people write checks for 25 to 50 thousand dollars to get a book written and published. The only thing they wrote was the check.

Many famous authors have said 95% of publishing success is marketing, selling, and promoting your book, just 5% is writing it. They are right. I have so many stories about the world of publishing that I plan on writing a book about in the future.

So here is what you need to know. Self-publishing is far more profitable, most of the time.

On too many occasions I sold my manuscripts to traditional publishers. In some cases, I had to buy my rights to publish them again or sue them to get them back.

The problem was after they printed it once, they refused the request for a second-print run unless I paid for the whole thing. I found that to be very unacceptable.

So, I found a good lawyer who wanted a new expensive car... and I ended buying him a nice boat too. Eventually, I got my rights back, but only after the publishing house went out of business.

In today's world, you can self-publish, put it up on the Internet, and keep most of the money for yourself.

That's probably how you found this book and many, many more. Hey, my iPad has a couple hundred books on it. I travel often, and I love to read, so this was a great alternative to carrying half a case of books on vacation.

The self-publishing transformation is in high gear because we're at a great time when tablets have reached critical mass; connectivity is universal, and people want to share their knowledge.

Thus, the time for every author to consider self-publishing is upon us.

Content control. Self-publishers can control what's in a book and its length. They only answer to themselves for the content of their books.

Design control. Self-publishers can control how it looks and feels. They control the cover design. If you want French flaps, you can include them in the printed version. The author controls the look and feel of the interior from page one to the end.

Time to market. A self-publisher can get their book to market in less than a day once it's copyedited, and the cover is designed. Traditional publishers take three (more like six) to nine months to get a printed book to market, and normally they will not release the e-book version earlier than the printed version.

Revisions. Self-publishers can revise books immediately with online e-book resellers and printers that are working "on demand." This is very important in today's world because Internet marketing changes often, affiliate links change or get updated, and all this means that you have to make those changes too.

Traditional publishers can take months to fix errors because they only print revisions after they've sold off current inventory.

Higher royalty. Self-publishers can make more money. Amazon pays 35 percent to 70 percent royalty to e-book self-publishers. You are lucky to get 10 percent with traditional publishers.

Price control. Self-publishers can change the price of their book at will. For example, they can set a lower price to try to sell more copies, or set a higher price to communicate higher quality.

Global distribution. Self-publishers can achieve global distribution of their e-book on Day One. For example, Kindle Direct Publishing will list an e-book in one hundred countries. Apple's iBookstore reaches fifty countries.

Longevity. Self-publishers can keep their book in print forever. Traditional publishers stop marketing a book once sales decline.

You own your rights to your book. If you sign your rights over to a publisher, read and understand every single word and sentence in the contract. Hire a professional to explain it to you. It's expensive to get your rights back, and it might involve lawyers.

Control of foreign rights. Self-publishers determine who buys foreign rights and for how much. They can make more money because they are not sharing foreign-rights revenues with a traditional publisher.

Analytics. Self-publishers can receive real-time or near real-time sales results. Traditional publishers provide twice-a-year royalty statements—imagine running a business in today's world with two sales reports a year.

Deal flexibility. Self-publishers can cut any kind of deal with any kind of organization.

Oftentimes, when I am invited to speak to a group at an event, I can offer my books for sale in the back of the room, include them as part of the package, or deliver a link to a discount for my books and products; thus, I do not have to haul around suitcases full of books and products.

Traditional publishers only sell to resellers, except for bulk sales of printed books to large organizations.

Control of the marketing. If your book is seasonal, like summer vacations, holiday shopping, how-to books for graduates, or ties into a seasonal sport like football or golf, then you are able to control the marketing, message, timing, and CRO (conversion-rate-optimization).

Summary: Publishing is your secret key to getting booked. My files are filled with published authors who deliver speeches for big money. Don't ignore this and don't put if off. Get to work on your plan and make it happen.

CHAPTER 15

Do You Think I'm Sexy?
The Secret to Success and
10 Recommendations for Working with
Agents and Speakers Bureaus

1. First… work on yourself and develop your brand. The agents at bureaus and management companies will be able to book you more often if you are well-branded. Give the agents and bureaus a great story to tell about you. It will be a great advantage if you are a recognized expert in your field.
2. Invest in you and your marketing materials. This will make it easier for agents and bureaus to sell you effectively. And remember, a great media kit and good, branded videos for the agents to use go a long way in getting you bookings.
3. Invest in the relationship with the agents at the bureau. Work with the bureau team to make the deal happen. The bureau sales teams appreciate a speaker who is committed to working with them to customize a proposal for an event and do it effectively.

Example: We just had a client ask for an RFP (Request for Proposal) that included speakers, celebrities, and entertainers. This client preferred a female speaker who knew direct selling or had experience with it, and possibly speakers who knew some Spanish. This was for two dates and a large budget. The agents worked on composing a request for availability to 11 potential speakers.

We asked to confirm their availability.

We asked them to approve budget compatibility. 30K for both dates, plus expenses.

One date was in Washington D.C., and the other in Las Vegas.

We included the exact dates.

Then we asked if they believed this was a good fit for them, and why.

Then we asked them to send list of direct selling companies they have worked for or had experience delivering presentations.

Lastly, we asked for suggestions and recommendations that would help us sell you to this 70% Hispanic and 90% female audience. Any assistance would be much appreciated.

Some speakers replied with a one-word answer: YES. So much for collaboration and the power of teamwork.

Others sent confirmation of their availability and approval of the budget, along with a list of direct selling companies they have worked for. A couple of them sent well-worded paragraphs that we could use in our proposal to the client to position them as worthy and more than capable.

One said, I know a little Spanish, and I would be willing to buy a Learning Spanish Program if I earn this date.

Guess whom we promoted hard? And guess who earned the bookings?

Yesterday, a DMC (Destination Management Company) called us at 2:15 PM. They need a proposal for a client today by 5 PM. That's often how it works. Some people treat it like they are ordering a pizza and chicken wings. It's frustrating.

We delivered a proposal by 3:30 PM, and within 24 hours we received verbal confirmation they are moving ahead with the booking. I asked them if they could provide some feedback regarding why we were chosen over the competition.

The representative told me, "Your proposal was part of a group of over 10 proposals we offered." She went on to share, "Your proposal addressed all their concerns, needs, topics, budget, and included a list of how the speaker was qualified for their industry, how he could connect with the audience, and exceed their expectations. With the list of testimonials and 'live, demo, sizzle reel', it was a slam-dunk."

It's nice when things work out. You hear me say this a lot because we both know it's true. Hard work, efficiency, and dedication will take you far in this business.

4. Be flexible on travel. Sure, first-class travel is nice. Expensive dinners, room service, and presidential suites are nice too. Top of the line rental cars and limos are nice as well. They are all very nice, but in this economy you need to be fair and reasonable.

Most frequent travelers can upgrade travel on a coach ticket (even a cheap one) and still fly in the front of the cabin. Some clients will pay for the fancy extras, but in other cases they are unable to pay for them because of corporate by-laws, government regulations, or policies they have to follow.

More times than I can count, we had heated discussions that involved the difference between expectations and reality with speakers and entertainers. We don't recommend those people anymore. Life is short. Play fair.

In my case, and in the case of dozens of our best "A" List people, we offer an inclusive fee that covers all air and ground transportation, meals, and gratuities.

The client covers lodging with their room block. That way the client knows what to expect and there is no BIG surprise after the event.

There is one caveat, I learned the hard way that you need to make it very clear to the client that the contract needs to be signed and the deposit check cleared 35 days prior to the event, or there is no inclusive fee option.

If I find this may be a deal breaker or cause a misunderstanding, I put it in writing and require confirmation of receipt with the proposal.

One more tip if you want to show some love for your agent. When you book an event and agree to a flat fee for travel, in most cases you might not spend the whole thing. I am speaking from experience, because I am a frequent flyer, and I know how to buy tickets right. In every booking, I do the accounting after the date and determine how much is left over. Sometimes it's under or over a hundred dollars. Sometimes it's a bit more or less. I send a handwritten thank you note to the agent every time, along with the accounting on the expenses. If we had a positive result on the bottom line, I send them 50%.

It's nice when things work out. It's not going to break my bank, but it sure lets them know you care about them. It builds loyalty and trust, and that is more likely to guarantee future recommendations and bookings.

5. Communicate with the agents promptly. Let me reiterate this; communicate with the agents promptly. Here is why that's so important: They build their reputation on good, fast service and having access to current information on your fees and availability. They want to make the deal happen, and timing is critical. Your **best practice** is to make it your policy to promptly return calls and respond to email! Check your messages three or four times a day. If you are too busy to follow-up, hire a competent personal assistant or virtual assistant and train them well with your policies and procedures.

This last part is important. Here's another from my closet full of stories:

A popular speaker hired their unemployed, college-educated niece to run the office.

The niece had a degree in art history and was a nice person, but not qualified to do the job, nor did she have the desire to learn it.

It cost the speaker several big dates with us. When I spoke with other agents, they said the same thing. The speaker told me later it was a big mistake and very costly lesson on several levels.

The lost business and the lost momentum took years to rebuild. Some of the relationships with agents were destroyed, and most importantly, the damage to his family relationship.

6. Don't quibble, barter or quarrel over commissions. The name of the game for you should be maximizing revenues. Bargaining with an agent or a bureau over commissions is a guaranteed way to encourage their agents to find another speaker.

About 15 years ago, a speaker I had known for over 20 years came to me and said, "How about if I agree to pay you a higher commission to book me. In return will you manage more of the marketing?"

I was intrigued. He was a proven speaker with credibility, and he was getting ready to retire from his real job at a university he held for over 35 years. He had a nice nest egg put away, but he did not enjoy the marketing aspect of the business. By his own admission, he did not like doing it.

This speaker understood the economics of the business very well. He offered a 50% split on the speaking fees, so we were dedicated to promoting him when it was a good fit. He was always grateful for the bookings, and would say 50% is better than zero any day!

More than a dozen years ago, a bureau called me up to inquire about booking me for a specific event. They provided me with the details: over 200 people, 80% male, working in hi-tech sales all over the world. The meeting was in Miami, Florida.

They were planning to play golf, go deep-sea fishing, and visit museums. I explained how to position me with the group. I offered to play golf with them. Back then, I was almost a scratch golfer, so I was comfortable with that. Plus, I would drive to Miami and bring my own clubs to save on expenses.

I am a licensed boat captain, and thought maybe going out on the water with them might work. I have been in the art world all my life and I thought this was a great fit to connect with them.

Since this was our first time working together, I wanted to let her know what a good partner I could be for her. I gave her a customized outline that addressed each of the client's issues and concerns in under two hours.

Then I asked what she liked to earn in a commission, and she said the normal 25% rate, and I said, "Well, I am not comfortable with that."

She tensed up on the other end of the phone; I could feel her pucker factor edging up past 10. I said very sweetly, "I insist on gifting you an extra 10% because you earned it." She was silent, and then shrieked "REALLY!?!" She was shocked and overjoyed. That is standard operating procedure with me. Pay them more than they expect, exceed their expectations, and treat them like family. Guaranteed to earn this booking and future bookings. A friend's mother used to always say, "Don't bite the hand that feeds you, kiss it instead."

She did a very good job of selling me to them. We planned a conference call, and I stuck to the business side during the call. I asked them many questions about the group and the program, the points they wanted covered, offered some good suggestions about topics and timing, and a strategy to exceed their expectations.

We wrapped up the call. Two days later they contacted the agent to inquire about booking me for two more days so we could just hang out, fish, and play golf.

Then they called her back to buy some of my books and training materials.

They even invited my family and offered to cover all the expenses.

It's nice when things work out.

The agent made a very nice extra commission that day. She earned much more in commissions from spin-off work and product sales from that event with me over the next several years.

She made more than three times what she expected to make on this booking, and she became a raving fan for me. Like I said, it's nice when things work out.

Moment of truth: The hard and soft costs of running a bureau or management company have gone up significantly over the last 20 years. The cost of hardware, software, training, marketing, websites, labor, taxes, insurance, and much more have shrunk the profit margin.

If you want an independent team of agents dedicated to booking you often, treat them well and offer to pay them a bit more. The payoff will show up on your bottom line with more good bookings. Like my friend's mother use to say, "Don't bite the hand that feeds you, kiss it instead."

7. You can offer to participate in phone calls with the decision makers to close the sale and to prepare for the speech. In fact, I request it but never insist on it. My record was 16 client calls in a row where the client was interviewing many potential speakers for an event, and I earned the booking.

Once the client commits to the booking, it is wise to offer to do as many calls as the client wants. Willingness to go the extra mile makes a big difference, and most clients are reasonable and respect your time.

8. Be willing to reschedule a speech. Sometimes events beyond the client's control make rescheduling necessary. When the Persian Gulf War happened in 1991, we had to reschedule 61 dates. Only one speaker was bull-headed about getting paid for not doing the booking and refused to reschedule it.

It was more important to us to save the relationship with the client, so we paid off the speaker out of our profits. We gave the client a full credit towards a booking with a different speaker. Of course, this bull-headed attitude ended the speaker's career with us and probably cost the speaker many thousands of dollars in future income. Regrettably, that kind of shortsightedness is very common in the industry.

"In matters of style, swim with the current. In matters of principle, stand like a rock." – Thomas Jefferson

The agents, the clients, and the bureaus will appreciate you more if you are accommodating. But, put time limits on the reschedule option. Normally, a year or two works. Put it in writing and include your first right of refusal for scheduling conflicts.

After 9-11, we had over a dozen events that cancelled. Each speaker understood the situation and was willing to work with us and the client to reschedule the event in the future.

Sometimes, speakers have to cancel too. It happens occasionally. It is addressed in the contract they sign with us. One of our speakers lost his mother unexpectedly, and we were able to find a replacement in under an hour. One of the jobs in the bureau is to have "Plan B" ready in case a situation arises.

Another time a young speaker suddenly passed away. This speaker had many bookings scheduled and one of our former clients, Charlie, called us up for advice on how to proceed with the situation.

Now to be clear, they had booked several speakers in the past with us, but Charlie chose to not use the services of a speakers' bureau and had booked this speaker directly.

Since I was very familiar with the situation, as we had two bookings with the deceased speaker that had to be cancelled and, based on our contract terms, we had to notify the clients, process refunds, and work with the clients to fill the slots.

Our office referred Charlie's call to me. But before I took the call, I checked our future bookings list and did not see that event or booking in our system.

Charlie and I started out with the usual small talk, how's the family, played any golf lately, but then the conversation moved right to the issue of the big deposit they'd paid the speaker and how they could get a refund?

Charlie said, "My job is on the line here. This is a big chunk of our budget."

While I was empathetic towards Charlie's situation, I had to inform him since he booked this directly with the speaker and chose not to use the services of a bureau or agency that would have protected and insured his position and his money; he would have to contact the lawyer handling the speaker's estate. He would probably be required to hire a lawyer to file a claim and conceivably take it to court. It will undoubtedly be tied up in probate and perhaps take a couple years.

Groan. Sorry Charlie, too bad when things didn't work out.

9. Be a team player. Offer to attend receptions, sign books, do photo sessions, kiss babies, cut ribbons, meet with the press, promote the client, open the trade show, promote their future events, and offer to assist them with getting things done. This is an investment in your future.

If you spend some time at the meeting, you will see some ways to offer other services in the future. If you can avoid it, don't just fly in and fly out. Meeting professionals want to feel your commitment to their meeting's success.

10. You can earn spin-off business by just showing up and being good on stage. But you will build a great career, earn many loyal followers and a good reputation if you show up and offer to be a part of the team.

When you spend time at the meeting proactively developing spin-off business, your bureau partners will recognize it and respond positively to it. This kind of action also makes a statement about your commitment to creating a win-win relationship.

Summary to The Secret to Success and 10 Recommendations for Working with Agents and Speakers Bureaus: Go read this chapter again!

CHAPTER 16

The BIG Mistakes Most Performers, Public Speakers, Trainers, Authors, Broadcasters, Actors, Musicians, Icons, and Experts Make, and How You can Avoid Them

Here Are The Big Mistakes As I See Them...

- Lack of focus, i.e. trying to be a jack-of-all-trades, is the first big mistake.
  - Speakers, trainers, and every performer who offer programs on several subjects are never known for anything.
  - The author who writes in several genres is doomed to be known for nothing.
  - The broadcast journalist who does national and local politics, plus fashion, pro and amateur sports, the weather, and local stories about rescued animals will find it difficult to get promoted to bigger markets or the national news desk.
  - The musician who can play classical, rock, heavy metal, blues, swing, country and western may find session work in studios but will be challenged to build a loyal audience following them.
  - The public speaker who delivers talks on a range of subjects is not remembered or known for a topic.

Find the genre you love. Make sure it is in demand. Go after it with the passion and intensity of a downhill skier in the Olympics.

- Do your research first! Don't spend too much time becoming an expert on a subject. You may find out there is limited demand, not much profit to be had or the shelf life is short. Or worse, you may find so much competition that getting to the top is profoundly difficult.
- Avoid not having an effective marketing and public relations plan or failing to test it before you roll it out. Avoid not having a good enough one, and not executing it properly.
- Avoid not developing a loyal team of support people agents, partners, and advisors who share your dream of success.

(These are some of the people you test things with. See number three.)

- Avoid failing to make everything you do have purpose.
- Avoid failing to change to market conditions, requirements, demands and momentum.

This story makes the point: A well-known speaker with a good reputation for innovation and strategic planning put his career on hold to care for an ailing relative. While doing so, he took a consulting job with a client that required what little free time he had to share.

On paper, it sounded like a win – win.

However, he failed to stay in touch with his agents and speakers bureaus that represented him. He did not return emails and requests to deliver keynote speeches. He failed to update his website. His relative's illness dragged on slowly for three years.

His consulting job ended after more than a year, and he spent his spare time writing a book and training program about how to deliver a speech.

Hopefully, this won't come as a shock to you: We receive very few requests for professional speakers to deliver paid presentations on the subject of public speaking.

When he finally contacted me to give me an update about what he had been doing for three years, he announced with flair his desire to change his brand and focus to delivering keynote speeches about public speaking.

I had to deliver the bad news regarding supply and demand in the market. I told him, "Please don't take my word for it, call the other agents you work with and tell them what you told me and see what happens." Needless to say, he was very bummed out. It took him at least five years to try to get back to working, and he never could regain the momentum he once had in the market.

To be good you have to have two things:

First, you have to be great on stage when you deliver a speech, a presentation, a concert, a show, or any performance, including when cameras are pointed at you, like an interview in the media. It needs to be good, rehearsed, tight, dynamic, impactful, relevant, and more.

Second, you have to be really good offstage too. You have to be able to market yourself effectively and efficiently, run your business ethically, and build a reputation as someone good to work with. When you have proven that onstage and offstage you have what it takes to make it in this business, then you're ready for primetime.

I promised to reveal how agencies and speaker bureaus work... When you're done reading this book, you will know how the game is played, you will know what's expected of you, and you will know how to build and maintain long-term relationships with agents, promoters, and clients for many years to come.

Not long after I founded the company, a prominent speaker and coach who is a member of a prominent speakers' organization contacted us. He provided us with very good marketing materials. He looked like a very good fit for our client list.

Actually, he was one of the best ones we had seen in a while.

He was listed with other bureaus, had a long track record in the business and was good on stage. We, in turn, set into action a plan to contact at least a couple hundred meeting and event planners. We would appropriate people at companies to solicit business for this person.

In the first 30 days, our plan included three weeks of getting press kits and videos ready to send, and writing and testing phone scripts. Our plan included training the agents on who he was, what he offered, and all the fine points of how to sell him. We set up training with mock phone calls so they could practice the sales pitch and hone it and get comfortable with it.

Then we were sending out press releases, and identifying "A-LIST" clients with whom we believed he would be a good fit. I should point out here that he knew nothing about our efforts on his behalf, up until this point.

In the fourth week, we turned our agents loose on the market-place, and they made contact with over 300 potential buyers. We sent out 60 kits to those who were interested. I remember this like it was yesterday, because we usually get one-third or less, so with this kind of good response, so we were encouraged for his future with us.

Our investment at that point was more than several thousand dollars. I need to point out here this was pre-Internet days, and things developed twice as slow, and took much longer to make things happen. (I don't miss the good old days!)

On the 32nd day, a Tuesday morning, he contacted us with a mean-spirited, faxed memo stating awful things because we hadn't booked him.

Our senior team quickly met to determine how to proceed.

To get further clarification, it was agreed that I would call him since this was my project and I would seek further clarification from him.

It was right after our morning meeting to discuss proposals, bookings, and projects. It was right before our Monday lunch meeting, and our team was getting ready to continue working on this project for him after lunch.

Now I believe in running towards a problem, not away from it, so I called right away and got through to him.

I said, "I am in receipt of your memo, and I am seeking further clarification."

Then, I just listened. The coach proceeded to lay into me with a very unprofessional tone and flow of language that would make a locker room full of athlete's blush. He continued to yell and scream, rant and rave, huff and puff, and frankly, I was shocked by his tone and demeanor. In all my years of being an athlete, I only encountered one coach who was similar to him, and no one liked him or would play hard for him.

Once he ran out of steam, and while still huffing and puffing, he ended it with a question: "What have you done for me?"

After a long pause, I very quietly explained everything we had done for him in explicit detail. Upon completing the explanation, he said, "Oh, then carry on."

At that point, I had to make an executive decision. I determined that we don't need to be working with him. If he's treating his agent like this, it gives us great concern and reason to believe he would treat our clients in a similar fashion. He said, "Well, I would never do that to a client." And I asked him, "Oh, and what are we, the agents who represent you?"

There was a long silence, and then he said: "I guess I see your point." I ended the conversation by saying, "We will not be doing any future business with you. I hope your day improves."

His decision to behave like that may have cost him several million dollars. Not only did he destroy the relationship with our agency, but many others in the future. Remember, don't bite the hand that feeds you; kiss it instead.

I made the tough decision to cut our losses and move forward. But our losses were minimal compared to what they could have been. We were able to find different and better people who were as good, probably better, definitely more humble, respectful, and withstood the test of time.

Life lesson: Choose the people you want to do business with. Choose professionals who you would be proud to work with. One of my test questions is would I invite this person into my home for a family dinner? Can I trust them?

"Geography has made us neighbors. History has made us friends. Economics has made us partners, and necessity has made us allies."
John F. Kennedy

More than a decade ago, a young speaker contacted us with his media kit. Everyone in the office who saw it was excited. We all saw potential in different markets for this young person, so we agreed to do our due diligence. We sent someone to go watch them work in another city, and she came back with rave reviews about his performance on stage, and how professional he was with the client and the audience members before and after the show.

Then we call the people on his reference list and called other agents who represented him. He checked out great. We contacted him to request his permission to move forward, promote him to our clients, put him up on our website, and proceed with a plan to book him.

Within sixty days, one of our clients, who happened to be a school, contacted us and said they want to move forward and book him. We said, "Great. Let's confirm the availability with the speaker and we will contact you with the details and agreements."

At that point, we left a message with his answering service. A few hours later we heard back from him telling us, "Sorry, we have a problem." He went on to explain that he has a long-standing agreement with an exclusive booking agent who books all of his school business and we would have to give the booking to them. He went on to say, "You cannot book me for schools, ever."

So I said: "Oh, really?? When were you planning on telling us this?"

And he said, "Well, I am telling you now."

All our efforts, resources, time, strategy, and money to book him at schools had gone down the rat hole.

Here are the lessons from this. The owners, managers, agents, and assistants who work at agencies and speakers bureaus can pick and choose whom they wish to do business with.

If you have prior arrangements and you are working on developing relationships with other parties, let them know your terms at the start and put it in writing. This is a two-way relationship.

For the agents and marketing people: it is wise to let everyone you are working with know about the efforts and resources you are using on their behalf.

That issue could have been avoided with clear communication, but it tainted the speaker's credibility and we chose to not recommend him again.

"A smart person makes a mistake, learns from it, and never or rarely makes that mistake again. However, a wise person finds a smart person and learns from him or her how to avoid the mistake altogether."
Frank Candy

A few years ago, a popular speaker and former professional athlete, called to invite us to watch him work for an event in Orlando. The event was in 45 days. We were very interested. We put it on our calendar and agreed to do our best and show up.

He cleared it with the client and provided us with the date, time, venue, room number, client's name, and the topic. He also extended an invitation to join him for brunch after his presentation. I contacted him back to let him know two of our agents wanted to come and watch him work. He said great, go for it. So far, so good, right?

Well, the event was on a Monday at 10:30 am. I was over at the beach house for the weekend, about an hour and twenty minutes away. Instead of going to the office first, I drove straight to the event and our agents drove in from the office.

We all arrived at 10:15 am. We met in the parking garage and entered the hotel to look for the meeting room. We soon discovered he was on stage and just wrapping up. We heard the last two minutes.

The agents were furious for wasting their time (remember, they are on commission) and this left a bad taste in their mouths. They had clients requesting proposals and deals to close. They were not happy to waste a morning driving in heavy traffic to get stood up, and they left.

I waited for the speaker to finish selling his books and DVDs. Then, he informed me that he wanted to go up to his room to put away the unsold products, change clothes, and that he had to make some calls, and finally, an hour later, he met me in the restaurant for brunch.

He explained that the client changed his start time a few weeks ago, and he forgot to notify us of the change. OOPS.

Our business is very detail oriented and our success, or lack of it, depends on attention to details and good time management.

This speaker wasted our time and resources and in turn, along with the brunch, left a bad taste in my mouth. Plus, each of us had spent a couple hours in the car, and the hotel charged us twenty bucks to park each car. Not a good way to start a partnership.

Now, for the record, for every story I share with you like this one and the others, there are twenty or fifty stories about great speakers and wonderful experiences. I hope you agree the stories from the bad experiences make good points for you to ponder, and I hope you consider them valuable lessons.

Summary: Focus on subjects that are in demand now and in the future. Develop a good plan with a qualified team of trusted advisors. Be willing to change with the times, technology, and trends.

P.S. These mistakes are common and can be avoided with focus and effort. I suggest you review the chapter called: Someone to Watch Over Me How to Select, Build and Maintain an Advisory Board. It's - The Secret to Faster Success.

CHAPTER 17

I Did It My Way - Mastery

In the spring of 1984, a close friend (the family lawyer, who was like our consigliere) came over on a Friday afternoon and gave me a copy of the current Esquire Magazine. He recommended I read the cover story about Mastery.

Well, I read it, and then re-read it, and have since read it many times over the last 30 years. Like many people, as I get older, my perspective on life changes, but I don't regret growing older, it is a privilege denied to many.

The article draws on a Zen philosophy of achievement, long-term success, and fulfillment. It clearly stated how to identify and deeply experience joy and fulfillment in our daily lives, and it outlined the disciplines required to lead and manage yourself and the people around you.

Reading that article inspired me to make some important changes: to study leadership and mastery extensively, continue my work and travels, and to focus on things that really matter.

Buddha said: "When the pupil is ready, the Master appears."

Actually, I question if it is really a Buddha quote, but all that matters is you cared enough about your success to buy this book and read this chapter.

So I will do my best to live up to your expectations, and I deeply thank you for coming to learn.

Mastery is an extremely pleasing feeling when one finally gets on top of a new set of skills, and then sees the light through the new door that those skills can open for them.

Mastery is comprehensive knowledge or skill in a subject or accomplishment. It could be leadership. It could be driving a car, bus, boat, motorcycle, plane, or train. It could be playing a musical instrument or delivering a keynote speech. If you are reading this book, then I hope you take seriously how important it is to master what you will be doing on stage in front of audiences. Just being above average will not sustain a career.

Master/Expert. Masters and experts create new knowledge. They invent new and better ways to do a job, and they can teach others how to do it. They are truly unique individuals and seek to learn in unique and personal ways, primarily through collaboration, research, and problem-solving.

Mediocrity is such an unfulfilling form of existence. Why settle for just okay when you can be so good that the world is left ogling at your skills?

Though being the best will take time, determination, and practice, it's a consummate feeling.

Here are tips on how to get there, starting now.

The fact of the matter is that you will always be you.

You can do something about your weight. You can do some things about how you look and dress. You cannot do much about your height, so work with what you have.

"When I was a child, my mother said to me, 'If you become a soldier, you'll be a general. If you become a monk, you'll be the Pope.' Instead, I became a painter and wound up as Picasso."
Pablo Picasso

When you're someone you're not, eventually that person fades away, and you return to you. This is the person you'll be working with, so get to know yourself!

"Accept who you are, and revel in it."
Mitch Albom, "Tuesdays With Morrie"

You'll be more comfortable in your own skin. You'll be a better person, a better friend, a better boyfriend/girlfriend, husband/wife, and employee. You'll be a better everything. You'll be less stressed, and you'll be more confident. You'll know what you're working with and how to work it.

"No one can make you feel inferior without your consent."
Eleanor Roosevelt, "This is My Story"

Know that you are not what people think of you.

"And no one will listen to us until we listen to ourselves."
Marianne Williamson

You can reinvent yourself, and perhaps the time to do that is now.

"Go confidently in the direction of your dreams.
Live the life you've imagined."
Henry David Thoreau

Find yourself and work with it.

"Somehow I can't believe that there are any heights that can't be scaled by a man who knows the secrets of making dreams come true. This special secret, it seems to me, can be summarized in four Cs. They are curiosity, confidence, courage, and constancy, and the greatest of all is confidence. When you believe in a thing, believe in it all the way, implicitly and unquestionable."
Walt Disney

That's what Steve Jobs meant when he said this at a Stanford University commencement speech: *Your time is limited; so don't waste it living someone else's life. Don't let the noise of others' opinions drown out your own inner voice. You have to trust that the dots will somehow connect in your future. You have to trust in something, your gut, destiny, life, karma, whatever. This approach has never let me down, and it has made all the difference in my life. The only way to do great work is to love what you do. If you haven't found it yet, keep looking. Don't settle.*

No matter how old you are now. You are never too young or too old for success, or going after what you want. Here's a short list of people who accomplished (against the odds) great things at different ages...

Helen Keller, at the age of 19 months became deaf and blind. But, that didn't stop her. She was the first deaf and blind person to earn a Bachelor's of Arts degree.

Mozart was competent on keyboard & violin from an early age. He composed from the age of 5.

Anne Frank was 12 when she wrote "The Diary of Anne Frank."

Nadia Comăneci, a Romanian gymnast, at age of 14, scored seven perfect 10.0 and won three gold medals at the Olympics.

Pele, soccer superstar, was 17 years old when he won the world cup in 1958 with Brazil.

Elvis was a Superstar by age 19.

John Lennon was 20 and Paul McCartney 18, when the Beatles had their first concert in 1961.

Jesse Owens was 22 when he won 4 gold medals in Berlin 1936.

Beethoven was a Piano virtuoso by age 23.

Isaac Newton was 24 when he wrote "Philosophiæ Naturalis Principia Mathematica".

Roger Bannister was 25 when he broke the 4-minute mile record.

Albert Einstein was 26 when he wrote "The Theory of Relativity."

Michelangelo created two of the greatest sculptures "David" and "Pieta" by age 28.

Alexander the Great, by age 29, had created one of the largest empires of the ancient world.

J. K. Rowling was 30 years old when she finished the first manuscript for Harry Potter.

Amelia Earhart was 31 years old when she became the first woman to fly solo across the Atlantic Ocean.

Oprah was 32 when she started her talk show, which has become the highest-rated program of its kind.

Edmund Hillary was 33 when he became the first man to reach the top of Mount Everest (highest mountain in the world).

Martin Luther King Jr. was 34 when he delivered the speech "I Have a Dream."

Marie Curie was 35 years old when she got nominated for a Nobel Prize in Physics 1903.

The Wright Brothers were 32 (Orville) and 36 (Wilbur) when they invented the world's first successful airplane.

Neil Armstrong was 38 when he became the first man to set foot on the moon.

Mark Twain was 40 when he wrote "The Adventures of Tom Sawyer" and 49 years old when he wrote "Adventures of Huckleberry Finn"

Rosa Parks was 42 when she refused to obey a bus driver's order to give up her seat to make room for a white passenger.

John F. Kennedy was 43 when he became President of the United States.

Henry Ford was 45 when the Ford Model T came out.

Leonardo Da Vinci was 51 years old when he painted the Mona Lisa.

Ray Kroc Was 53 when he bought the McDonalds Franchise and took it to unprecedented levels.

Dr. Seuss was 54 when he wrote "The Cat in the Hat."

Chesley B. "Sully" Sullenberger III was 57 years old when he successfully ditched US Airways Flight 1549 in the Hudson River in 2009. All of the 155 passengers aboard the aircraft survived.

Colonel Harland Sanders was 61 when he started the KFC Franchise.

J. R. R. Tolkien was 62 when "The Lord of the Rings" books came out.

Ronald Reagan was 69 when he became President of the United States.

Jack Nicholson was nominated for 12 Academy Awards and Won three times, in 1976, 1984, and 1998.

To quote one of my dearest friends, the late Orville Hissom, at age 81, "Age is just a number, but being young is an attitude..."

You might say, those were people that had some kind of advantage in life, yet I expect they were normal people with purpose who believed in themselves, they ignored the critics as best they could and pressed on with the philosophy of "WHY NOT ME?" SO IT BEGS THE QUESTION, WHY NOT YOU?

THE ANSWER LIES WITH IN YOU!

Summary: Why not you? This is your show, your future, and your life. I only offer advice and strategy. I have never met two people who are exactly alike, so it is safe to say everyone needs a plan that fits with their values, dreams, goals, risk tolerance, budget, and desire to make it happen. Make your life a masterpiece. I wish you well.

CHAPTER 18

Come Fly With Me – Partnerships, Values, and Choices

Back in the late 90's, I was hired to keynote a national conference for over 500 engineers. I decided to check out the room on the afternoon several hours prior to the sound check we had scheduled.

I had been traveling all day to get to the event, so I was wearing casual slacks, running shoes, and a golf shirt.

As usual, I was hoping to hook up my laptop and test everything. Plus, I like to rehearse in the room I'll be presenting in and walk the whole room to look for dead spots or problems while it is still fixable.

The doors to the room swung open shortly after I arrived. A couple people came in and started unloading large, heavy boxes of manuals, goodie bags, and cases full of equipment. They must have assumed I worked for the hotel, and a tall woman with two walkie-talkies and a big, four inch thick, three-ring binder and clipboards, started barking orders at us to unload the boxes from the dolly's and go out to the truck in the parking lot for more boxes and equipment.

Now, I have set up my lifetime share of trade shows, meetings and events, and I have walked a many a mile in many meeting planners' shoes. I know how stressful and difficult it can be. Most of them have the attributes of a super hero. They hide their rage and despair because they love the work but dislike the carnival life - and are trying not to flame out too quickly because of the job.

Now, I am a team player and a strong guy. This was not an unreasonable request of these people. Plus, it was clear they were dazed, under-staffed, and very frazzled like most meeting planners who are overworked, under-appreciated, and underpaid.

I just smiled and said: "Yes, of course, I'll take care of it right away." For the next couple hours, we moved heavy boxes into the room and unpacked them. Then, she told me to set up the workstations in the back of the room. She asked us to rearrange some of the furniture in the room and place the manuals at each setting. I was working so hard and fast I broke a sweat.

Just as I was putting down the last row of manuals on the front table, the A-V tech walked in and asked her if the keynote speaker was here for the sound check. She answered in a very edgy and annoyed voice, "He is not here yet, and he is late. Can you come back later?"

He said: "Well I can try, but we are really busy and shorthanded tonight."

At that point, I spoke up and quietly said to him, "I'm Frank Candy, your keynote speaker, and I am ready for the sound check."

Well, you could have heard a pin drop in the room. This lady turned colors, from pale white to crimson red like the carpet, and tried to talk. She seemed to be going through the five emotional stages of grief: denial, anger, bargaining, depression and acceptance. Not surprisingly, all that came out was aaaaaahhhhhh. I smiled a kind smile, stuck out my hand in a friendly gesture to shake hers, and said, "Hello, I am Frank Candy, your keynote speaker for tomorrow morning."

At that point, she looked very confused, fraught, and embarrassed as her eyes were rotating in opposite directions and searching the four quadrants of her mind in an attempt to process this. Again all that came out of her was aaaaaahhhhhh. She had to sit down.

The AV tech and I went through the sound check. I secured the location of the equipment and soundboards in the back of the room, we confirmed the location of the volume controls, power supplies, backup mic, extra batteries, confirmed the emergency exits, the light switches, and double-checked the lighting set up for the front and back of the room and stage, while she just sat there and watched with her jaw on her chest.

After we were done she came up to me and started to apologize, and I said, "Not necessary or required. We are a team. I am doing my job, which is assisting you to make the best show it can be. What's next?"

Wires need to be taped down; workstations need turned on and tested. We ended up being in there until after midnight decorating the room in a very cool locker-room motif.

Well, the next morning when I met the president of the company he was very complimentary. He mentioned a conversation he had with the meeting planner about my extra efforts, and our relationship was off to a great start.

The keynote was about teamwork, and I hit a home run with my stories about being a part of winning teams, going the extra mile, and teamwork. I was booked on the spot for three meetings in Maui, Mexico, and Miami. The president and meeting planner both wrote glowing testimonial letters for me that I have parlayed into more speaking engagements, and I read them if I want a boost or forevermore us as a weapon against self-doubt.

Best practice: Be a part of the team. Walk a mile in their shoes, be humble, be willing to do what-ever-it-takes to make the entire show a success, and play to win.

But it reminded me of something my parents instilled in me from a child:

You should always be kind. Everyone you meet is fighting a battle you know nothing about. Be kind. Always.

One of my friends and co-founder of the National Speakers Association, Cavett Robert said:

"The road will never be easier — it is up to us to be stronger.

Our profession is not easy. It belongs to those strong and courageous people who dare to dream, have faith, expect the best, and are willing to sacrifice.

Strength always flows from adversity. Troubles, trials, and sacrifices have always constituted the fertile soil for growth. If you will take time carefully to review your life, you, as everyone else, will realize that you make your greatest progress in life during times of discouragement and challenge.

Summary: Be a team player, walk a mile in the other persons shoes, and look for ways to make this a better world and place to live.

CHAPTER 19

89 Lucrative Profit Centers For Speakers, Experts & Entrepreneurs - The Secret Combinations to Massive and Passive Income

1. Speaking for fees on business topics

2. Professional speaking in specific niche markets to build the brand and get spin-off opportunities

3. Delivering motivation and inspiration to thousands from the platform

4. Speaking in Breakout Sessions

5. Delivering content and or strategy and recruiting new customers at industry events

6. Speaking representing your employer

7. Delivering product information at industry events

8. Be a presenter who sells products and/or services from the platform

9. Traditional mainstream books with a publisher and Self-Published books and E- Books

10. Audio Books

11. Audio Books combined with content (workbook) from a speech about the book

12. Audio Programs delivered by CD and digital online, used both as products and as marketing tools

13. Video Trainings - As a way to deliver the same content yet at a higher price

14. Multi-Media Programs **Multimedia** is distinguished from mixed media in fine art; by including audio, for example, it has a broader scope.

15. Audio / Video / CD / Printed materials sold together as a program

16. Workbooks (These can include many different formats and are very profitable)

17. Individual, standalone training tools, not part of other products

18. Coaching Programs provided by you or by others under your direction

19. Mentoring Programs

20. Apprenticeship Programs

21. Offering one-on-one advice + group training to protégés

22. Public Seminars that you promote or with a promoter

23. Upsell attendees into higher priced programs There is a very precise formula for this

24. Train-the-trainer Programs

25. Selling licenses and teaching others to present your material and use your products

26. Corporate Training Programs

27. Your material licensed for use company-wide

28. Presenter at Large Events (thousands of people) with the intent of selling your product

29. Multi-Day Boot Camps

30. Intensive weekend trainings by you and your handpicked experts

31. Tele-boot Camps (this is done by phone or webinar, over a couple or several days)

32. Same intensive content delivered by phone over several weeks

33. Hourly Consulting for projects (It's recommend to sell blocks of time – three hours or all day)

34. Long-Term Consulting Contracts (could be weeks, months or years)

35. Consulting to meet a long-term goal for large corporations or government departments

36. Ongoing consulting for a monthly or annual fee, this is uses more for private coaching and consulting in an advisory role.

37. Spokesperson Contracts

38. Your reputation and expertise utilized to sell products & services

39. Licensing your products, services, and content distributed by others under your name or theirs

40. Infomercial Product

41. Product designed to sell on the radio or via television infomercials

42. Home-Study Courses

43. Multi-media product format designed to be a complete system in a box

44. Teleseminars

45. Seminars conducted via one or more group telephone conference calls

46. Weekend Retreats

47. Personal growth weekends designed to inspire change

48. Promote your weekend and offer to sell the video and audio recording to the ones who did not come to it.

49. Your subscribers receive monthly digital recordings or CDs and/or Newsletters

50. Printed or electronic newsletters, white papers, or guides, for free or for profit

51. E-zines (the electronic magazine format)

52. Monthly or semi-monthly communications, either for free or paid subscriptions

53. Radio shows to promote your brand, career, services and products

54. Television shows to promote your brand, career, services, and products

55. Everything from short segments to syndicated radio show to TV specials

56. Partner with Philanthropic Foundations as an outlet for your message or for other causes

57. Media Expert, position yourself as the go to expert in your field

58. Providing regular content to news organizations

59. Syndicated Column

60. Your articles appear regularly in periodicals

61. Private-Label Magazine

62. Magazine with your name and title, but produced by others for your use

63. Ghostwriting

64. Co-Authoring

65. Writing for others with cover credit or not

66. Branded Retail Products

67. Hard and soft goods produced for retail consumers with your logo or name

68. Mini-Books (these have become very popular)

69. Smaller versions of your book with cut-down content used as premiums

70. Rights - Yours

71. Foreign, serial, broadcast, syndication and derivative product rights

72. Rights - Other People's

73. Acquiring and re-selling other experts' products and content

74. Special Reports

75. High-priced information on a specific business topic

77. CD-ROM / DVD Training

78. Typically sold for use as a training tool, but can be used for marketing, too

79. Counseling Services

80. Usually one-on-one, personal growth counseling

81. Adult Professional Education or CEU's

82. For industry associations or for consumers through local seminar companies

83. Compiled Reference Guides

84. Directories and other compilations on useful forms, resources and material

85. Software

87. Your own or templates designed for use with off-the shelf applications

88. Trade Association (Start your own!)

89. Operated by you to assist a specific industry group

Here are some bonus ideas

90. Industry Conventions & Trade Shows with revenues from workshops and trade show booths

91. Certification Training

Summary: You have many options. Pick the one(s) that are best for you. Start with one, develop a plan and a budget, and determine who you will need to hire or partner with to do it right. Discuss it with your Executive Advisory Board (See Chapter 26) and make sure you understand the strategy required, risks, profit potential, and timelines. In the long run the answer will lie within you.

CHAPTER 20

The New Normal In the Real World of Public Speaking

Here is what you need to know about the new normal in the real world of public speaking for money and the opportunities in our new normal and new world order global economy.

There are many people traveling around and speaking at events and conferences all over the world. For some reason, how they were chosen and why they were chosen is the secret you want to know.

I am not going to candy-coat my view of the market today, but first let's review some history.

In the 1970's when Richard Nixon, Gerald Ford and Jimmy Carter were Presidents, the speaking industry was mostly under-developed territory like the wild, wild west and mostly occupied by popular authors, sales trainers, and business icons.

Prior to the first Gulf War, when Ronald Reagan was in office, or what I call the 'easy to make money days' in this, or virtually any business! Speakers with a good story, and decent platform skills earned some very nice money. The ones with very good platform skills, strong branding, or a Super Bowl ring, Olympic

Medal, or a best-selling book were in high demand. Plus, when the speakers used phrases like synergy, strategy, TQM (Total Quality Management), best practices, or leverage, they were paid more.

The speakers with great branding and relevant information like competitive market intelligence, were flying all over (and racking up lots of airline frequent flyer miles) to speak at meetings, conferences for corporations, non-profits and trade associations, franchise groups, network marketing groups, and many government agencies on the federal and state level.

After Ronald Reagan left office, George H. W. Bush Sr. was elected. During his campaign, he promised not to raise taxes. Then, after he was elected, he raised taxes. Subsequently, the economy went into a downturn, and the press portrayed him going fishing and golfing. He was voted out of office after one term, but while he was the President he was the first U.S. President to use the phrase "New World Order" in a speech.

William "Bill" Clinton was elected to the presidency because he kept saying, during the campaign, "Change vs. more of the same" often, along with building a new and better economy. Remember, "It's the economy, stupid!"?

At this time, computers were changing our business environment in many ways and companies like Microsoft, IBM, Intel, Dell and Apple, and many were taking off. The Internet, which had been around since the 1980's, (no, Al Gore did not invent the Internet) was quickly becoming a popular commercial application, and soon every speaker was expected to have a website and eventually, a demo reel online.

It was at that point the "change" Bill Clinton was talking about was happening in a big way. So many people found themselves unemployed and unable to fit into the new world order of technology in the workforce. So they dove into the speaking profession. I watched many thousands come and go.

Well the economy took off in part because of the technology boom in America, and there were no big wars, and if you stayed up with the technology, and could lead people and manage the massive change, or tell people how to do it, you were pretty popular and probably in demand as a public speaker.

If you used words and praises like, empowerment, value added, client focused, think outside the box to win-win, and take it online, you were paid more than the speakers who told stories from the soon to be very popular book series called Chicken Soup for the Soul that came out in 1993.

At the speakers' bureau, our focus was spread across over a dozen markets for speaking and training:

Corporate
Manufacturing
Retail
Agriculture
Automotive
Aviation
Transportation
Franchising
Health Care
Pharmaceuticals
Finance
Travel
Trends
Insurance
Entrepreneurial start-ups
Direct Sales Organizations

The hot topics were:
Leadership
Teamwork and team building
Marketing
Business growth strategy
Mergers and acquisitions
Human resources
Stress management
Time management
Sales including B to B, B to C, and channel selling
Service
Branding
Information Technology
Internet
Trends
Globalization
The environment
Politics
Investing

The education market with elementary, middle, and high schools, colleges and trade schools, plus in-service days for teachers were big business. So were graduation ceremonies. Most of the schools were budgeting for speakers. For an agent who specialized in this market, they could make a very good living by just focusing on booking speakers for schools.

Actually, there are some agents who still book schools almost exclusively, but their market share is less because most of the schools budgets are less.

The federal, state, and local governments, along with law enforcement were hiring speakers for their meetings before the economy crashed in 2007 and it required a specialized skill set to work with their demands and requirements. We became proficient at it, and we did pretty well.

At the speakers bureau, we were all cross-trained to serve any market, but it took a couple years of training, and working in the market to really understand it, and know it. Usually, we would start off an agent in one market and train them on each one over time. Most of us were a specialist in more than one market, plus specific topics, and an expert on the core competencies of specific speakers, trainers or entertainers.

As an example, in my case, because I have a background in marketing, business development, technology, the performing arts, sports, and a couple engineering degrees, I specialized in high-tech, business, business authors, sports legions, astronauts, and entertainers.

Well, the NY Stock Exchange and NASDAQ took off in the 1990's with an irrational exuberance that expanded the investments in Dot Coms, and inflated stock prices so high that when the bubble broke it hurt the economy and the country badly.

They said a correction was due, and I saw bumper stickers that said, "I want to be irrationally exuberant again."

We endured another election and this time Governor George Bush from Texas won it with a Supreme Court decision.

Fast forward

Then the unthinkable happened. On 9-11, terrorist destroyed the twin towers in New York City and the Pentagon. It changed our world, our country, and our industry, forever.

Prior to 9-11, there were days when a speaker could do two events in different cities on the same day and still fly home and sleep in their own bed. Back then, we could show up at the airport less than 30 minutes before the flight was going to leave and make the plane. Everything changed, including our bottom line profit margins.

My personal best was speaking at a breakfast meeting in Central Florida, leaving my car at the Orlando airport, and renting a car to drive one-way to Tampa to speak at a luncheon at a hotel ballroom near the airport, then boarding a jet to Atlanta, where I delivered a dinner speech, and finally flying back after 9 pm, getting in my car, and driving home to spend the evening with my loved ones.

On July 18, 2014, I was in New York City to keynote the Annual Chairman's Conference. I flew in early because I wanted to go to the 9-11 Memorial and Museum at Ground Zero. I will state my own experience was sobering and very intense. I consider it as the continuation of the massive national healing process, and the attempt to understand this horrific tragedy. My sincere congratulations to all who worked so hard to design and rebuild this beautiful complex.

After 9-11, the economy struggled to come back, and we went to war for the first time in over a decade.

People were afraid to travel and canceled many meetings.

I had a flight on September 14th that was virtually empty. So were the airports, it was a very bad feeling. I was booked to speak for a small group of top sales performers, and what was supposed to be a one-hour session became two hours with most of it being an open discussion about 9-11 and how to move forward. They were in shock and frozen in fear.

The economy and the country recovered slowly under the leadership of George W. Bush Jr. and Dick Cheney. At this time, many people were leaving their jobs to become speakers because it looked easy. The speaking industry was maturing, and the competition for work intensified. At that point, if you were established and well-branded, things were going well for you.

With two wars raging, the national debt continued to climb and irrational exuberance took place once again, this time in the housing market, and the result was the economy experiencing the worst recession since the great depression.

Wall Street recovered, but Main Street has not. It will take some time, and like Grandpa used to say, "You must play the cards you are dealt."

Many speakers were desperate for any work, so the competition for speaking opportunities became much more fierce, and any job was bid on and negotiated by reducing the cost of speaking fees, plus products like books and training tools being sold at cost, or even below cost to raise cash and reduce inventory.

Several speakers told me they would rather lower their fees to work and pay bills, and sell their products at a loss than pay the cost to store and insure it in a warehouse. So the race to the bottom was off and running at a blazing speed.

In simple terms of supply side economics, the supply of speakers increased and the number of opportunities decreased. The country lost millions of jobs, and so many more people jumped into the speaking business, and so with these factors, the race to the bottom became very ugly.

The four common denominators remained constant: Branding, marketing, good platform skills, and reputation, they matter.

Then the country elected Mr. Obama based on his campaign slogan, CHANGE.

Many people were hopeful. I understand because while he was campaigning, he was delivering very good speeches, and saying what people wanted to hear.

Unfortunately, his policies encouraged people to not seek employment or retraining to get employed. Today, there are over 1 million U.S. job opening that require specific skills, and no one to fill them.

Our bridges and roads are crumbling, and there is no plan to rebuild them. Our airports are relics; our infrastructure is crumbling, and leadership and politics in Washington has myopic vision and is stuck in serious gridlock.

America needs retraining and jobs that rebuild America, and get people off the government subsidy, and free money handouts.

The current system rewards people for continuing to make bad choices. One of the ways would be to put forth a plan to grow the business community with jobs that really matter.

We are in desperate need of good leadership with long-term vision, and all I can say is, watch for is my next book.

Within a month of becoming the President, Mr. Obama seriously injured the meetings industry, the speaking industry, and small business community by threatening to audit all business meetings.

Mr. Obama crushed the service jobs industry and stuck a knife in the heart of its business community in the first quarter of 2009 after the media reported on an executive incentive meeting for AIG.

He went on TV and said: "Companies need to be on notice that we will not tolerate frivolous business meetings in places like Orlando and Las Vegas."

This is an excerpt from my newsletter, the Motivational Minute in 2010:

Since September (2008) when the economy went south, a bunch of meetings throughout the world have been cancelled or postponed. A reason that is popping up more and more is, "We don't want to look bad, in the eyes of the public." According to many clients, this is passed to them from the Marketing, PR, and Legal departments. "All of a sudden, holding a meeting is viewed by the public as a waste of money."

I was troubled to hear that Sen. Kerry has introduced legislation that bans Troubled Assets Relief Program (TARP) recipients from hosting, sponsoring or paying for conferences, holiday parties, and entertainment events.

Hard working employees are losing the chance to grow their companies and celebrate their success at a time when the media is intent on beating home a message of doom and gloom. Sales conferences are being cancelled at a time when they need the inspiration and motivation the most. Remember, "Nothing happens until somebody sells something."

Cancel a meeting, and you stop the flow of funds to other industries such as air and ground travel, hospitality, food service, printing, production, entertainment, training and development. Bailout funds are intended to get the economy moving, yet any effort to spend a dollar is held with suspicion and even contempt.

One of the things the media and this administration have done is put fear in the minds of business people. Our clients told us if we have a meeting, and we hire speakers, and reward our people with perks for doing a good job, and let them play golf, the press will release a report or story, and we will be slimed, which is obviously bad for business, and our shareholders.

One of the best ways that business gets done in America is with face-to-face meetings and conventions. Unfortunately, AIG was singled out by the media for having executive incentive meetings for their top performers on the west coast. Then, most companies became paranoid that they would get bad press for holding meetings with their people.

The result was companies became terrified of being scrutinized in the media and being audited by the government, so they stopped booking speakers and holding business meetings.

Cancel all meetings was the cry!

They stopped meeting and growing, and the ripple effects were profound throughout the entire supply chain in the service industry - hospitality, food and beverage, catering, transportation, travel, A-V Support, professional speakers and trainers, and so much more. Many people around the country crashed and burned.

It's no wonder several cities with the deepest recession problems were also cities dependent on business meetings and business tourism. Orlando and Las Vegas were hit the hardest!

The U.S. Chamber of Commerce has complained about a "tsunami" of new taxes and regulations under Obama since 2010.

TUESDAY · APRIL 15, 2014

OBAMA HAS PROPOSED 442 TAX HIKES SINCE TAKING OFFICE: Since taking office in 2009, President Barack Obama has formally proposed a total of 442 tax increases, according to an Americans for Tax Reform analysis of Obama administration budgets for fiscal years 2010 through 2015. The 442 total proposed tax increases does not include the 20 tax increases Obama signed into law as part of Obamacare. "History tells us what Obama was able to do. This list reminds us of what Obama wanted to do," said Grover Norquist, president of Americans for Tax Reform. The number of proposed tax increases per year is as follows: -79 tax increases for FY 2010 -52 tax increases for FY 2011 -47 tax increases for FY 2012 -34 tax increases for FY 2013 -137 tax increases for FY 2014 -93 tax increases for FY 2015. Perhaps not coincidentally, the Obama budget with the lowest number of proposed tax increases was released during an election year: In February 2012, Obama released his FY 2013 budget, with "only" 34 proposed tax increases. Once safely re-elected, Obama came back with a vengeance, proposing 137 tax increases, a personal record high for the 44th President.

Currently, the corporate tax rate is too high, and many claim it prevents job creation, and while it could be lowered, it will require political will and leadership with vision.

So that was a history lesson of the meetings industry and speaking opportunities.

To complicate the market further, many associations changed their business model to shorter meetings, and they changed their sponsorship packages that in the past included a banner on the wall behind the keynote speaker that they paid for, to eliminating the professional speaker, and selling one or multiple 20 or 30-minute slots to a vendor or a couple vendors.

It makes sense from a budget perspective, but long-term it could be a poor decision. Growing the membership should be the top priority of an association. They do this by providing services, education, community, advocacy, resources, networking, inspiration, and career advancement. Much of this happens at their annual meeting.

For many decades, people have attended business meetings. In my experience what they remember most is not the tasty meals, or the wonderful hotels, or entertainers, but the number one thing was the way the speakers made them feel, and the content, insight, strategy, message, and emotional connection they created and delivered.

Reflecting back they would say: "Remember the meeting with that amazing speaker astronaut Rick Searfoss, or the meeting with four-time Super Bowl Champion Rocky Bleier, or the six-time Emmy winner, Ross Shafer?" Now that opportunity has flat-lined, but it is not dead.

In my study of the market over 30 years, I have watched attendance at industry meetings across the board rise and fall based on the success of the speakers and overall evaluation of the meetings. There are some meetings I will attend again because they have a reputation of bringing in great speakers and others who will never see me again because they lack good quality speakers with content.

Obviously I am in favor of hiring as many very good speakers as possible, but I don't control the market forces.

"Each player must accept the cards life deals him or her, but once they are in hand, he or she alone must decide how to play the cards in order to win the game." Voltaire

The stagnant economy has changed buyer's positions about speaker fees.

So has the free speaker.

Every time there is a downturn in the economy, budgets get cut, the line item for paid speakers is crossed out, and speakers without strong branding reduce fees to compete.

This is why some $20,000 speakers are going for as low as $5,000 or less.

Another trend is the market forces have forced the maturing of the speaking business.

Since the beginning of the speaking business, speakers could use guerilla marketing to get bookings, and if they were good, the phone rang, and more bookings appeared. It was almost like magic, except magic is done with smoke, mirrors, and misdirection.

Between changing buyer expectations and the increase of new speakers, more resources are needed to start and produce a profitable speaking business.

Meeting and event planners, and the people they answer to who write the checks, are willing to pay top money for the speakers they really want.

The four common denominators remained constant: Branding, marketing, good platform skills, and reputation, they matter.

There is another competition issue to throw in the pot and stir up.

The Baby Boomer Generation is retiring, and many former Presidents, CEO's, and executives want to leverage their previous success into big speaking fees. Makes sense. I have heard some of them and they are highly skilled men and women and very, very good.

These smart and experienced people understand business, branding, and marketing, and they have the money and resources, plus they have high-level contacts, so they will control some of the top-level market share and get some of the top bookings.

Many top executives from Corporate America are booking slots in programs to position their companies as market leaders.

Another trend over the last decade has been a big rise to in public speaking training to corporate executives and government officials.

Public speaking is considered a customary leadership skill; so up-and-coming leaders use keynotes and panel discussions to increase their industry profile.

Public speaking trainers, consultants, speechwriters, and public relations executives are making are doing very profitable business by making these placements.

Organizations get free speakers for their events, so their bottom line is better.

Another trend is booking speakers to deliver a live broadcast to a meeting. Our speakers' bureau was blindsided by one of these online tech companies, when we brought them into the C-Suite of our client, to discuss using this approach with our speaker. Turns out they went around us and promoted using their primary investor as the speaker, and they would do it all for free.

Sometimes things don't always work out. We found a new tech company to partner with that we trust.

For the last three years, meetings have been increasing but what they do and what they buy is scrutinized like crazy!

An executive with a pharmaceutical company that we have been booking top level speakers for since the 1990's told me in 2008 they had under 300 pages of government regulations, now they have over 1,200 and it keeps getting worse.

While attendance at meetings is increasing, yet, the extras like paid speakers, golf, deserts, and perks are scrutinized and reduced or eliminated from the budget.

Some of the meetings are using online networking as a strategic advantage, and offering education online. This online option is not new. I was doing conferences with NASA starting in the 1990's, but back then it was really expensive.

Now, online meetings are rather common and the technology is very inexpensive, almost free, in some cases, and this becomes a critical skill for communicators to develop and perfect. I am not saying you must do it or perish, rather, it is another way to communicate, and a profit center you might consider. The answer lies within you.

Audiences want in-depth learning from people who have been there and done it.

They depend on speakers with authenticity that will give realistic value in an interactive format.

Social media will plague the speakers and experts who fail to deliver a high quality, valuable message, and failure to deliver creates a deep hole to crawl out of.

For the established speaker, they need to re-package their background and topics with a strong brand for the ever-changing, multi-cultural, multi-tasking, multi-generational workforce.

So, several speakers were asking me if the ten, fifteen, and twenty thousand dollar speaking engagements are still out there. The answer is yes, we are still getting requests for them, but it is harder to book them.

The speakers earning those engagements are getting them because they have a strong brand and are strategically executing a solid marketing plan, and working the new social media channels and platforms that new buyers consider important.

Usually, when a group is considering a speaker, they do not want the typical sales conversation. You have on opportunity to make a great impression and close the deal with these sharp people. You must know what to say at the right time or you are eliminated from the list of contenders.

Before the economy ground to a halt, the speakers with stories had a purpose.

You still need your story about winning the gold medal or a championship ring or overcoming the odds to thrive. Your story adds a framework, and creates an important emotional experience.

But your story alone will no longer justify a big speaking fee.

Dwell on this for a while: How can you apply their big idea and combine it to include your story to support it. Make sure you convey to the buyers how the audience can use that idea to advance their objectives and purpose.

Look, if you are in the speaking or training business or an agent in the business of booking people, then allow me this observation, we are all actually in the marketing and communications business.

Meeting and event planners in the new world order of things do not have it easy.

In the new world order, selecting a speaker or performer is a treacherous undertaking like offering to be a test dummy for a car crash or a test subject for a new drug. It may cause nausea and vomiting, allergic reactions, drowsiness, insomnia, water weight gain, lower back pain, itching, blood clots, excessive body odor, diarrhea, loss of bladder control, anxiety, sleeplessness, drowsiness, chest pains, and even a heart attack! All of these symptoms and many more are caused by stress. And hiring the wrong speaker can cause lots of stress.

The meeting planner, the event planner, the company executive, the committee chairman and even the entire committee may have a say in who is booked - and they better be right.

The new world order includes high expectations by the attendees, and the professionals who have been hiring speakers for over 20 years have stated that the pressure is higher than ever.

One of the things they do to create a safety zone by contacting several speakers' bureaus and requesting proposals from them.

They can look through the proposals and quickly highlight any speaker who looks good and disregard the ones who do not fit their criteria or expectations.

Over the years, I have observed so many speakers say the wrong thing in voicemails and interviews with prospects or committees. And they do some very inappropriate things in emails too.

The clients and the decision makers are concerned about four things:

What will you give, and do for the audience?

Do you give off any clues that you would be difficult to work with?

Do you fit in their budget?

Are you clear and professional about your expectations and expenses?

Smart authors and speakers who understand the big picture will address these issues with a detailed sales dialogue and analysis with the people on the line. In the past, I have had calls with two to 32 people interviewing me on a call. 32???

The one with 32 people I imagined was in a conference room, and they had an amplified speaker system. I made sure I did not speak too loudly, or fast. I stood up, stayed focused on their purpose, only answered the questions I was asked, I did not lecture or ramble on, and ended it very pleasantly. Half an hour later they called me and said I had won their hearts and minds, and they wanted to book me, and I won the opportunity over 13 other people they were considering.

After we had completed the paperwork and before the pre-event interviews, I was talking one-on-one with my contact that was in that room of 32 people. I asked her why they chose me.

She said, "You were focused on our needs and issues, you said the right things, and we felt you were a safest choice." I also learned I was the last one interviewed. The take away lesson I learned was when you find yourself in the interview situation and up against your competition, work to get the last interview.

It's been over 10 years since I booked a free event in return for exposure. I rarely see the value in it these days.

As I stated back in chapter 2, in my observations people have either been arrested or died from exposure.

It doesn't serve you or your brand to do things for free. If you are doing an event with the opportunity to sell something, that is a different business model, and I get it.

If you choose to do something pro-bono for a charity you like, fine, those kinds of things matter, but they rarely build your brand, or move your career forward.

If you have expectations of selling your books, audio programs or training packages, you MUST know the group's expectations ahead of time.

Over the years, I have met or connected with so many authors and speakers that do not even know their real value in the marketplace. Most of them have built their business on referrals, and their referral base is evaporating like smoke in the wind from three factors, 1) Baby Boomers, are getting older and retiring and dying. 2) Loyalty is becoming less and less a thing we can count on. 3) All the rules of branding, marketing, positioning, public relations, promotions, advertising, and selling are changing fast.

They must re-package their expertise with an in-demand brand, based on what buyers really want.

Summary: In the final analysis, thousands of speakers are booked every day for money, and you need to ask the right questions like: How did they do it? And WHY were they chosen?

The four common denominators remained constant: Branding, marketing, good platform skills, and reputation, they really matter.

The authors, entertainers and public speakers who will get booked often for good money are the ones who build a relevant, strong, valuable and reputable brand, they will continuously innovate to improve and execute their marketing plan and keep publishing books. They will consistently improve their platform skills and develop original material, to keep up with the sharp young and savvy senior audiences, and they will build and protect their reputation because it does matter in the new world order.

CHAPTER 21

Develop The System To Find Sponsorships, Stay booked, and Live Well

Booking speeches one at a time is difficult, time-consuming, complicated and an expensive endeavor.

What if you could book 10, 25, or even 50 events with one client over the next three of four months? Imagine going on a speaking tour of the country, or the world, and going first-class, staying in fine hotels, eating great food, meeting wonderful people who adore you, and autographing thousands of books along the way.

Are you living the dream? Keep reading.

Sponsorship is becoming a preferred method of marketing, and due to its success, it is growing rapidly every year.

Over the last 20 plus years, I have been involved in sponsorship opportunities, and assisted other clients, agents, and speakers in partnering with telecoms, Internet providers, office supply stores, home improvement stores, hospitality groups, airlines, car and truck rental companies, training and consulting groups, professional associations, and good causes to assist the less fortunate in our society.

Prior to that, I worked partnerships and sponsorships with health clubs, sports equipment, food companies, pet supplies, transportation, and racing, to name a few.

PETERBILT MOTORS

Presents

Keynote Speaker – FRANK CANDY

Here is what you need to know:

Businesses are wisely opening up their pocketbooks for sponsorship because today's world likes innovative, emotional connections in marketing.

This is a growth industry and your odds of success in getting the first "test agreement" are better today than they were 10 or 20 years ago.

Yet, it is far more difficult to get the second commitment for a longer-term option. Here is why, in one statement, it is more complicated.

One of the reasons sponsorship is a growing trend is simply, follow the money. Budgets for meetings and speakers keep getting cut, but there is money in other departments for marketing, promotions, public relations, and advertising.

People who choose to seek sponsorship, and do it successfully, will research the markets, the industries, and the process first. The truly successful ones form a team, choose a leader, establish objectives, set big goals, and establish a plan with a strategy.

Over the years, I have consulted with many people and organizations, and time and time again made their investment in my services pay off with positive results.

We were able to get them on the fast track sooner by:

- Reviewed their branding, research, strategy, and plans to optimize them, and to increase their impact and effectiveness.
- Working with them on their proposals and making them more relevant.
- Coaching, drilling, and preparing them on their live and multi-media presentations and pitches.
- Making introductions for them to the right people who could open doors and make decisions.
- Increasing their success ratio.

There are several factors to consider:

First and foremost is the "risk and reward" factor. As a speaker, athlete, author, entertainer or famous expert, you take the risk of being linked to a product or a service that is in conflict with your values and/or brand.

When a sponsor enters into an agreement with a seemingly good person who gets bad press for making unscrupulous decisions (or might just be in the wrong place at the wrong time), the media goes crazy, social media is all abuzz with the juicy gossip of a potential scandal, then someone yells "breach of contract" (or worse) and the lawyers and public relations professionals swoop in, and there's a bunch of yelling and noise, sparks, and smoke, and when it clears, the agreement is very different or done.

In the 1980's, Michael Jackson entered into an agreement to promote Pepsi in TV commercials. These Pepsi commercials also played in movie theaters in-between new movie previews. And they sponsored his music tours for a reported 1.5 million dollars, which (he claimed) he donated to charity. When the allegations of Michael's improprieties exploded in the media, Pepsi dropped him, and reportedly lost 500 million dollars in sales.

It was also rumored that he was asked if he drank Pepsi and he said "No." That didn't help either.

Celebrity scandals and professional athletes fill our headlines and airwaves with gossip and drama. Sponsors are looking for the squeaky clean, all-American people to link their product to. There is the exception in the case of "had a transgression and entered a recovery program" story as the media loves a good come-back story.

Music groups from rock, jazz, blues, classical and virtually every form of music can partner up with sponsors for their tours.

Even some white-collar criminals earned sponsorship after paying their debt to society and re-entering the community, finding themselves funded by mutually beneficial groups. On occasion, they have even made movies about these criminals.

There are many stories like this to consider. Most of them have some good lessons behind them.

As you are reading this you might be asking yourself, do I need to be a pop star like Brittney, or a sports superstar like Tiger or LeBron, or a movie star like Jennifer, or a media mogul like Oprah or Trump to get sponsorship? The answer is no, not that big, but you need to have a platform, a following, and some notoriety for doing something people consider relevant. A well written, promoted and popular book is a very good place to start.

2. You need to do the research and background checks and make sure the right topics about values, reputation, expectations, and results are discussed and brought out in the open.

3. The Three "ROI" factors. ROI can stand for Return on Investment, Return on involvement, or Return on Innovation.

Return on Investment: In most cases, the sponsor is going to invest, time, money and resources in you to be a voice, face, and image for them. Just watch a NASCAR race when a reporter points a microphone at a driver, and he or she rattles off a fast falsetto of names like beer or soft-drinks, home improvement stores, shoes, coffee, detergent, restaurant chains, retail stores, oil companies, car manufacturers, clothing chains, and pharmaceutical companies, while wearing a racing suit and every square inch is covered with sponsor patches, along with the hats, the cars, the pits, and pit crews.

There is an old movie that stars Robert Redford and Willie Nelson called "The Electric Horseman", if you want to watch how one of the scenario's play out, watch the movie. It's a good story, has a wonderful ending, and the scenery is very nice. Another old classic movie worthy of your time on this matter is "Tin Cup". I consider both movies required research for anyone who hires me for consulting on a sponsorship project, because it helps them understand the dynamics on several levels.

Return on Investment is the incremental sales growth for each dollar of advertising or sponsorship funding. A high return usually means that the strategy is working, while a low or negative return may require a re-evaluation of the marketing strategy.

A company may need to change its core message, or advertise on several media platforms to improve the effectiveness of its advertisements. For example, even a small shift in the ad budget from radio to television or from print magazines to the Internet may improve the return on investment.

The sponsor wants to see a positive result in sales, client acquisition, market share, profit, and consumer behavior.

It's to your advantage if their marketing efforts are not up to expectations because you may offer a chance to improve things.

For instance, a good speaker and author who specializes and customizes speeches for the building trades, and delivers proven, and successful programs to statewide and national building associations, could enter into an agreement with a sponsor such as a chain store that sells home improvement supplies, and possibly a paint supplier to the store, and perhaps a plumbing supplier, and equipment distributor who channel sells their line through the store. It looks like a wise move on paper.

If you have an MBA in finance, perhaps a law degree and a popular book on the industry, entering into an agreement with the financial institution, and/or a software company might work.

If you have a degree in healthcare, and you wrote a popular book on the industry, it might be a good fit to enter into an agreement with a pharmaceutical company, national health care provider, or even both if there is no conflict of interest.

Do you see a pattern here?

Return on Innovation:

As I mentioned above, the company spends money on media to promote their product. They are always looking for better ways to promote their products and services.

My definition of the process of innovation is creating something out of thin air or making something better.

Over the years, I have delivered and presented at many conferences on the subject of innovation. I share stories, processes, processes and experiences using good innovation by changing the way people think, act, and shift paradigms.

Many times, sponsor's paid for my appearance and my expenses. Plus I brokered deals for other speakers that included giving their books and products to the audience members, thus improving the experience for the group and the profit for the speaker.

Raising the bar to show a Return on Objectives

Companies can measure the "return on objective" in several ways. If the objective is to change consumer behavior, a company could conduct a telephone or online survey to track brand awareness, ability to recall the effectiveness of a speaker's message and impact, or the advertising messages and purchase intent.

Or after a speech by the author, athlete, or expert, the group fills out evaluation forms that are designed to measure retention, impact, and possible changes in viewpoints or attitudes.

Companies could also measure the response to sponsorship and advertising messages by calculating changes in website visits, clicks on Internet ads, store traffic and sales.

For example, a retailer like a bookstore chain could measure the change in store traffic and sales of specific products, after a book signing, and perhaps a presentation on the day and week after event.

When I was doing more of this type of promotion, I learned how to trade for display ads, billboards, and combine them with multi-media from radio shows, TV appearances, and Internet ads and postings.

The point is I went above and beyond what they expected to demonstrate that I was the best partner for them by setting big goals, developing a plan with a strategy to cross promote the brand and products, developing multiple ways to measure the effectiveness, and making it happen.

I showed them what they were not counting and measuring, and by doing so I was able to increase my value to them.

Companies can measure the effectiveness of online advertisements in different ways, such as tracking the number of clicks on their Internet ads, social media "conversations" referring to particular ads and website visits.

Return on involvement: All the parties are now playing in the same room, so this is where in the pre-planning phase the expectations for involvement are played out in-front of the audience, cameras, media, Internet, and it needs to be done right, and done well. The show must go on, and it better be very good, or the lights will go out, as they say on Broadway.

In my case, I always tried to measure it in points, like keeping score in a game. Every time I shook someone's hand, I was sincere, looked him or her in the eye, and made a connection with them. Each book I autographed and personalized to them, each question I answered, every meal I shared, I tried to make the most of the emotional connection. My focus was building a fan base one person at a time.

Virtually every day we witness rudeness by movie stars and athletes, and it lowers their desirability ratings for fans, movies, and TV studios and sponsors. Nobody's perfect and everyone has a bad day, but when it is time to show up, my goal is to play nice and raise my score.

The choice is yours; the answer lies within you.

Here are a few more tips:

Finding the right fit. This is not easy but if you do your research on the front end, in virtually every case you will save time, money and resources.

The "timing" factor. Sometimes the powers in the universe don't cooperate with our grand plan. Bummer. I missed a meeting in NYC because the flight was cancelled due to weather delays. I was able to "attend" the meeting with a conference call from the airport in Florida.

As it turned out they had two questions for me. I answered both honestly and the first one flawlessly. The first question was how would I measure the results, and measure success?

The second question crushed my chances of working on this project. You want to know the question right? They asked me if I used the product. I told the truth; I said, "No, never in a million years." They asked a follow up question, "Why?" And I told them.

But before I ended the call, I left it on a high note by thanking them for their consideration, offered my services for other opportunities, and wished them well.

Three things happened right after the phone conference. 1) A big snowstorm hit the east coast and all flights were grounded for days, and I was still in warm and sunny Florida. 2) They called me back in four days to explore working on bigger and better projects. 3) We found a project we could work on, and it was more profitable and interesting than the first one.

You need to know the game and the rules before jumping in.

If you've sought sponsorship in the past, then you understand how connecting with the right person in the right place at the right time and the right place is so important. You may have been expected to jump through many hoops just to get your foot in the door, only to learn your target is not the best fit for you. Better now than later down the road.

It's tough work to get an audience with a potential sponsor, much more so if you want the most mutually beneficial relationships.

Sponsorship enables you to proactively reach the right people and create results that matter, and provide more exposure and more options than you ever thought possible.

If you are going after the big client, you might be advised to go through the public relations department or the marketing department.

The meeting or event planner is in a different department. Got it?

So I "tested" this chapter by sending it to the advisory board, and several high-level people for their consideration, opinion, approval and endorsement. Some of them came back with the magic question, "Where do you find the clients?"

Take a look at who is sponsoring events now. You can go to a sporting event and see many signs and banners, you can attend just about any function and the venue, building, arena or event is tied to a sponsor. What would NASCAR be like if they had no sponsorships?

Here are three examples: Healthy food is very popular. If you were an expert nutritionist and popular author, you could look to partner with growers, processors, distributors, or retailers or a farmer's market.

If you were an expert on industrial safety, specializing drilling for oil, you could partner with oil companies.

If you were a safety expert on cars or aviation, there are companies who would welcome the opportunity to partner with you.

If you were an expert on advanced learning and education, you could partner with many companies because that market is wide open.

Summary: Sponsorship is a popular and growing opportunity for the right situation. You need to know the game and the rules before jumping in. You need to have a platform, a following, and some notoriety for doing something people consider relevant. A book is not required, but it sure does help. Study the market, do your research, and form a team; choose a leader, establish objectives, set big goals, and establish a plan with a strategy, and possibly hire a good consultant to get you organized and aligned with potential sponsors.

Make sure you agree with your sponsors on how you will measure and justify their continued investment in you. Play nice, think long-term and look for ways to bring more and more value.

CHAPTER 22

The World of Grants And Changing Lives

Can you imagine someone giving you money because you have a good idea and a plan to make it happen?

The world of grants is complicated and not for the faint of heart.

Here is what you need to know.

Primarily grants come from private foundations, companies, and government agencies. The majority of the time the grants are awarded to non-profit groups.

There is a process, and procedure, rules and regulations, it has its own set of terms and is very technical. Don't be scared off. I read that hundreds of millions of dollars went unclaimed last year from just private foundation grants. Does this mean you can write a grant for something frivolous and they will give you a ton of money with no strings attached, so that you can go throw a great big party? No way. Everything has a price.

Where do you start: If you are a speaker, trainer, author, expert, inventor, artist, creative designer, or have a good idea that might have a positive impact on society, for which you would like to obtain funding, then maybe this possibility would be worth pursuing. I have been there and done it. Mark my words, it is not easy.

Here are a few things I learned along the way. Government grants come with all kinds of accountability. They are scrutinized very closely, and they should be, because it is taxpayers' money they're spending. Read the Chapter about doing business with the Government, it will give you more insight.

The media closely analyzes them so almost every week articles are published about some procedure or process that was violated or questioned. Often there are accusations in an attempt to hold the parties accountable.

Companies and corporations have their own agenda, and if it is a good fit, and you can play by their rules, then it might be a good decision to move on it. Also, companies will fund research for creative and innovative ideas that have a solid plan.

Then there are the private foundation grants. In many cases, they have specific interests and directives they must follow to award grants.

There are many books that cover the topic in much greater depth and more details.

Check the website www.publicspeakingformoney.com/books for recommendations.

The one thing I have observed over the years is there is an art and science to acquiring grants, and some people devote their entire careers to being grant writers. Once you get the first grant, and you prove to be a worthy partner, then securing the next grant becomes easier, and receiving the next grant becomes much easier to obtain.

Recently, I was consulting with a person who was looking for angel investors. I asked him if he had considered pursuing a grant. He was not aware of the possibilities that the grant community might offer him.

Once he pointed out the obvious benefits his plan had for serving the public welfare, with public transportation, reducing vehicle traffic, moving many more people than cars, generating electricity instead of using it, generating carbon credits, and the conservative break-even point in less than 10 years I was excited for him. He has a very good idea, vision, and a plan.

This appeared like a very good opportunity to earn grants for funding, design, building, equipment, operations, maintenance, and marketing.

The three sources listed above may be interested in his opportunity.

Thousands and thousands of grants are awarded every year for great projects and scholarships. There are some websites that list some of the crazy ones like a grant to a person with the best recipe can earn $5,000 in college scholarship money? Simply be a vegetarian high school student who promotes vegetarianism in your school or community, and you could earn a $1,000.00.

The Bill & Melinda Gates Foundation, at its 2014 "Grand Challenges" annual global health research meeting held this year in Bangkok, Thailand, announced it had donated more than $10 million worth of $100,000 grants in support of 104 scientific projects highly unlikely to have received funding through more traditional agencies or donors.

The national Center of Charitable Statistics reported in 2010 that there are more than 120,000 private foundations in the United States alone, citing their source as a 2010 IRS master file.

I watched a friend's son go through four years of college with no debt, paying for it with grants and scholarships. Today he is very successful, due in part to his grant-seeking abilities where he developed the skills to research, follow directions, fill out the paperwork, and follow through with his best intentions.

Please note that foundations generally give to nonprofits with 501(c)(3) status. If you don't have tax-exempt status, you might consider finding a nonprofit to work with or act as your fiscal sponsor. These might help you qualify for more funding.

It might be an option for you to consider crowdfunding if you have an idea and model to make it work.

Summary: Grants require a strategy, the desire to study and understand how to work within their parameters, a whole lot of persistence, and the good attitude of never giving up. Grant money can change how you operate, and allow you to influence people on a massive scale. I have pulled back the curtain to give you a quick view of the possibilities. Is it the right thing for you? The answer lies within you.

Do the research and invest the time reading a few good books on the subject. You might consider getting in touch with us to explore the possibilities or consider hiring a consultant with the expertise you need.

CHAPTER 23

Doing Business With Government
IS Good Business

Over my career, I have booked many speakers and myself with governments and agencies in the USA, England, Canada, Jamaica, Mexico, Europe, South America, and the Far East. I have worked with other speakers and speakers bureaus as a consultant to assist them to bid on, and earn government business. Booking work with the government is achievable and fun. However, it is not easy and is usually complicated.

Here is what you need to know.

Welcome to the world of acronyms. OMG (OH MY GOSH!!!) Get ready for acronym hell!

Each department, bureau, division, and group is different. I could fill a book with interesting stories about mountains we had to climb, and flaming hoops our agents at the speakers' bureau had to jump through to earn the bookings. Then I could write a sequel describing what it took to get paid, and how many things were required to have in place, and being very flexible, not to mention how I had to bite my tongue so hard I tasted blood!

I have several imperative things to do when working with all clients: ask, listen, and focus on exactly what they want and need, and how to deliver it, and how to get paid.

Each time you will hear, "we do things our way" and you must be willing to step-up and play that way or it's unlikely you will be able to earn the business.

Our policy has been to get at least one person on our side within the government or department – this person has been with them for a long time, knows how things work, and how to get things done. In my experience, the more horizontal and vertical contacts, the better.

I call them our internal advocates. They are like a sponsor for us and will be a campaigner for us throughout the process.

On our side, I will assign a point person for the event with the qualities of persistence, patience, and great attention to detail, and experience dealing with government bureaucracies. Putting an intern or inexperienced person into this position will be a regret-table decision.

Many years ago, I learned every "T" must be crossed, every "I" dotted, and every form filled out perfectly. Failure to do so will stall the process and with today's online process being accurate is so important.

The old cliché, you have to spend money to make money, comes into play here.

It requires more time, energy, and resources to get the busi-ness, and follow the steps and process of filings, hearings, inter-views, approvals, and then delivering the product or service, and getting paid.

It has been our policy to only work with speakers, trainers, and providers of services that understand and value our experience, talent, efforts, and the investment we have to make to earn and deliver government contracts.

Let me put this in very clear language for you. The cost of doing government business is high. The time, talent, energy and resources to make it happen, and to get it done is significant. Failure by a speaker, trainer, performer, service provider or partner who is unwilling or unable to recognize this and work with us on the process, and reward us for the effort, will be eliminated from any future opportunities.

In the past, when other agents have contacted me and were inquiring if I would be a good candidate for a keynote speech or a training program for a government group, I would inquire as to their experience dealing with this kind of client, process, and entity. About 75% of the time I believe we can work together. The other 25% of the time they fall short with the lack knowledge and/or experience required to make it happen.

However, the most important part of doing this is making sure you are a very good fit and can meet and exceed their expectations. The failure to do so can be very difficult to overcome, so don't say, "yes" too quickly, make sure your background, experience, topic(s) and delivery methods are a good fit for this event and group.

Experience is the name everyone gives to their mistakes. – Oscar Wilde

Here is more that you need to know: Every government agency, department, group and entity has its own secrets, acronyms and language. The more you learn and know, the better and faster you will become with the process.

First, I will share my comments on foreign governments, and then I will address the U. S. Government.

With the exception of a few foreign groups, they have been good to work with.

Occasionally we had to hire an interpreter; sometimes we had to jump through hoops to get the international wire transfers working, and sometimes they changed the schedule of the event which changed our speakers' travel plans and altered their schedule, but the client understood the additional cost of changing flights, and in more than one case were very kind and upgraded the speaker to first-class travel, so almost everyone was happy.

Let's take a sidebar here for a second. I just wrote, "almost everyone was happy" well, when our speakers bureau has to monitor, negotiate, and make changes to the booking on our end, it requires time and resources.

I hope we would all agree that time is money, and when we have to perform work over and above the normal expected workload, rarely are we compensated for it.

Most agencies and bureaus have good people who do this work, but they are on the hourly payroll, and if they have to stop working on a project, a proposal or an event, and get homed in and focused on a change with a different event, in reality, we are doing the work twice. Do you agree someone should pay for it? Point made. Since I have analyzed time sheets and the payroll for years, I know where the money is going and where the profit is coming from.

In the many years of doing this, I can count on my hand the number of times a speaker, trainer or entertainer has recognized our over and above efforts, and did something kind and meaningful about it. All of them are still working with us, except for one who passed away.

OK, back to foreign groups. If you book them, they can offer an amazing experience in foreign lands that are second to none.

Twenty years from now you will be more disappointed by the things you didn't do than by the ones you did do. So throw off the bowlines sail away from the safe harbor catch the trade winds in your sails. Explore. Dream. Discover. – Mark Twain

Here are a few more comments on working with and in foreign countries.

Get all the money in advance. This includes travel. This has been our policy for over 20 years. I don't see it changing. I lost count of the speakers who contacted me over the years, and asked for my assistance and advice on how to collect from a client, promoter or government in a foreign land.

First of all, the international legal system is very different from the USA. Threatening legal action makes them laugh like a silly YouTube video. I can remember only a few people over the years that were eventually paid by foreign clients. The rest of them gave up, and did not collect what was owed them.

The next recommendation is simplify your agreement with foreign groups, the simpler the better. And provide them with an easy way to wire the money to your bank account.

However, be sure to clearly spell out your lodging and ground transportation requirements. In most cases, you can ask for five-star accommodations and specify a Mercedes-Benz or similar quality vehicle with a professional driver. In a few countries, I requested security. In a few countries, I have politely required it as part of the contract.

If you plan on selling books, DVD's, or training materials, importing them might be a problem. Each situation is different so do your research. In some cases where there is enough planning time (e.g., if you are delivering a presentation in Malaysia), you could work with a printer to produce your books there and sell them there. It's been done.

Another issue is taxes. Each country is different, and each country might ask you to pay income taxes. If you earn the money in their country, they might expect a payment from you. Do your research in advance. You don't want to be sitting in a customs office or worse, trying to call your agent and lawyer. At the end of this chapter, I included some information on foreign travel.

Now, let's cover working with the United States Government, State Governments, and Local Governments.

In the past, if you were doing business with the Federal government, you needed a "CCR Registration". CCR stands for Central Contractor Registration.

The CCR is a government-wide registry for organizations that seek to do business with the federal government. The CCR collects, validates, stores and disseminates data to support a variety of federal initiatives.

Need to register? If an organization is not registered, it may register online at: www.ccr.gov

CCR has developed a user guide and a handbook to assist with the process. These publications include details on the information that will need to be gathered in order to complete the CCR registration process.

How long should CCR Registration take?

If an organization already has an Employer Identification Number (EIN) or Taxpayer Identification Number (TIN), it should allow a minimum of 48 hours to complete the entire CCR registration.

If an organization does not have an EIN or TIN, it should allow two weeks for obtaining information from IRS when requesting the EIN or TIN via phone or Internet. The delay is due to security information that is mailed to the organization.

When an organization registers with the CCR, it must provide: DUNS number.

The Data Universal Numbering System (DUNS) Number is a unique nine-character identification number provided by D&B.

If they do not have a DUNS Number. They must contact Dun and Bradstreet to obtain one.

U.S. Federal TIN. The Tax Identification Number (TIN) is the nine-digit number which is either an Employer Identification Number (EIN) assigned by the Internal Revenue Service (IRS) or Social Security Number (SSN) assigned by the Social Security Administration (SSA). If an organization does not have a TIN/EIN, contact the IRS.

CCR Point of Contact (CCR POC). This individual is responsible for maintaining the accuracy and timeliness of the information in the CCR registry for the organization.

Electronic Business Point of Contact (EB POC). This individual will have sole authority to designate the staff member(s) who may represent the organization to federal business systems. The same individual may serve as both the CCR POC and as the EB POC.

Marketing Partner ID (MPIN). During registration, organizations will be asked to designate a special password called an MPIN. Record and protect passwords.

U.S. EPA, Office of Grants and Debarment Tip Sheet for Registering with the Central Contractor Registration (CCR)

Important Notes:

CCR registration must be updated or renewed at least once a year, or it will expire. CCR will alert the CCR POC when it is time for renewal.

Organizations must ensure that all information contained in each database, the D&B DUNS, IRS and CCR databases, matches exactly.

For example: if an organization's address is 123 First Street in one database – entering 123 1st St. in another database will significantly delay the CCR registration process.

CCR uses data from the D&B DUNS number record for each CCR registrant's name and address. If, upon review, an organization finds that at any name or address information in their CCR registration needs to be updated, it will have to go back to D&B, which in turn will send the modified data to CCR where the CCR POC will have to accept it. An update will add a minimum of 2 days to the CCR registration process.

CCR also verifies with the IRS the Tax Identification Number (also known as the TIN or EIN) that each organization provides during the registration process. Because of this, it may take CCR 2 or 3 days after receipt of an organization's information, with a D&B-validated name and address, to finalize a CCR registration.

After the CCR registration is complete, CCR will e-mail a confirmation to the CCR POC.

Still with me? Hang in there, we are just getting started.

Most likely you will need a Cage Code from SAM. This stands for System of Awards Management.

Your CCR username will not work in SAM. You will need a new SAM User Account to register or update your entity records. You will also need to create a SAM User Account if you are a government official and need to create Exclusions or search for FOUO information.

The System for Award Management (SAM) is the Official U.S. Government system that consolidated the capabilities of CCR/FedReg, ORCA, and EPLS.

What is CAGE validation?

When you submit your registration in SAM, it is forwarded to CAGE for additional review and validation. If the data you submitted passes all CAGE edits, the registration will be processed automatically and returned to SAM with minimal processing time. This occurs for the majority of registrations. If the CAGE validation process identifies a potential anomaly when matching the key data elements you entered during SAM registration, your registration will be stopped and placed into a manual review process.

During the manual review, the CAGE office may need to receive clarification or valid documentation to support the data you entered into the SAM registration. If this is the case, the CAGE office will send an email to the Government Business Point of Contact requesting the needed information. It is important to reply to any emails sent to you by CAGE (coming from a "@dla.mil" e-mail address) within FIVE business days and supply the requested information or documentation.

In most instances, if the vendor provides the required information, the CAGE office is able to process registrations that require manual review within 10 business days after receipt from SAM.

If you are contacted and do not respond to the email within five business days, your registration will be rejected by the CAGE office and returned to SAM.

You will have to access SAM and save/submit on each page of your registration to resubmit to CAGE for processing. Once your registration is active, you can view your CAGE Code on the web by searching the active registrations in SAM, as long as you have not opted out of public display, or by logging into your account.

The "Help Manual" is 352 pages long. You can download it off their website. If you suffer from insomnia, this might be the cure you are looking for.

If you want to get booked by a government agency, they will require you to have a Cage Code. If you have a CCR registration, they will migrate your records from your CCR code, verify your standings with the IRS, and DUNS, the State you filed your corporation in, and the SBA. If it all checks out, you are good to go.

When I started working with the government, the Internet wasn't invented yet. Now that we have run headfirst into the information age, most of this can be done online. Each website requires you to set up an account with a unique login and password.

It's wise to keep all these numbers, login names, and passwords in a very safe place, like a fireproof safe, not the cloud, and have them at your fingertips.

It is also wise to have your Article of Incorporation handy. You will probably need them.

It is also advisable to have copies of your tax returns, and a really good tax professional with experience in these matters.

Another thing you should keep track of is every time you call one of these agencies; you will speak with very nice people on the phone. Keep track of the date, time, person's name, and if they have an employee number ID Number. Keep track of what was discussed, and the outcome. While you can ask them for a direct way to contact them to follow up, they rarely can offer that option. Sometimes they will give you a case number, be sure to keep track of that. I keep all my notes in a three ring binder then transfer them to an online database for future reference.

The process on the front end is challenging and tedious. It doesn't get easier. When you apply for the job or assignment, they will have guidelines for all your expenses, where you will stay, and how much you can spend on expenses like food, transportation lodging and handouts, and every detail can be micro-managed. In my opinion, most of the time, if you can ask them to agree to one, all-inclusive price, you will be better off.

After the event, you may have to wait for a few weeks or a few months to be paid. It is just how they do things. So get used to it and expect it. It is your choice to take it or leave it.

There's more. In this book and in my programs I have stated, "Hope for the best and plan for the worst." So here is what you also have to take into consideration.

By now you might be saying "REALLY??? ARE YOU KIDDING ME???' Well there is a fair amount of good opportunities for interesting work within all levels of governments. For the most part, I have found the people to be very nice, and the audiences have been very good.

The state and local governments are nice to do business with, yet they have their own set of guidelines that you will need to follow, so pay attention and ask all the right questions. Early on, I learned that they expect that you know and understand the rules like they do, so unless you ask, they won't tell you. It's common to not get paid in advance. Most of them, including schools and universities, receive state funds, and are therefore unable to pay in advance; it is in their by-laws or state charter.

Sometimes they ask if you will provide CEU's. A **continuing education unit** (**CEU**) or continuing education credit (CEC) is a measure used in continuing education programs, particularly those required in a licensed profession, for the professional to maintain the license. Make sure your background will qualify you to offer this. This will require you providing proof of your degrees and expertise on the topic and experience in the profession.

So those are the pros, here are some cons. You need to be looking at the future with 20-20 vision.

Government groups and agencies like The National Oceanic and Atmospheric Administration (NOAA) attempted to hire a magician to perform at a staff team-building event.

The Associated Press reported that in 2012, the agency posted a May 1 notice seeking a "magician motivational speaker" for a June leadership conference in suburban Maryland.

The notice said presentations should include "physical energizers, magic tricks, puzzles, brain teasers, word games, humor, and teambuilding exercises."

It also asked for the performer to create "a unique model of translating magic and principals of the psychology of magic, magic tools, techniques and experiences into a method of teaching leadership."

For these skills, the agency offered to pay $3,500. Clearly those who posted the notice should have first attended a PR workshop, as they had no idea how much fallout their solicitation would cause.

Congressmen and Senators called NOAA's plans "frivolous and ridiculous." House Science Committee Chairman Ralph Hall, R-Tex., gave NOAA Administrator Jane Lubchenco a week to provide a detailed explanation about past spending on magicians and comedians.

Sen. Scott Brown, R-Mass., in a statement, said, "This is a low point even by Washington's standards" and added, "the best magic that NOAA could perform would be to make this wasteful spending disappear."

The notice was pulled, and the magic booking was cancelled.

It's a long story. You are welcome to look it up and read about it if you have the interest.

In neither case were we talking about large sums of money by federal government standards, but that's not really the point. It's the taxpayers' money. And the media can earn ratings points by reporting controversy.

When any sum is associated with terms like psychic, magician, clown, mind reader or motivational speaker, the reaction might not be positive.

Aside from using federal monies to secure the services of unusual speakers and performers, the GSA and NOAA situations are not similar, despite what wild-eyed Representatives and Senators reason to think the plan was "frivolous and ridiculous."

What this make-believe scandal really underscores is something we already know –politicians will jump at anything they think will make them look like heroes in the public eye.

The details and context of the situation don't matter. What matters is that a charged term like "taxpayer money" can be leveraged for maximum gain, especially against all of those frivolous bureaucrats just itching to hire a clown, magician, motivational speaker, hypnotist or mind reader.

Those trying to make a capital case out of this should get zero credit for pretending to care about the facts.

So the points to take away are, be careful about how you brand, position, and market yourself. In the over reactive media world, and with the jaundice eyed media of today, the narcissistic attention whores could create situations that would make you want to run for your bed and curl up in the fetal position and not come out. You could make a seemingly innocent mistake, and it could blow up your career. I expect it will not get better in the future.

In Summary: Government business is good business. In over 40 years, their checks have never bounced. I continue to do business with them, and while it is complicated and tedious on the proposal and procurement side, the audiences are good and fun, and appreciate a great presentation. Consider securing and investing in good advisors or consultants to assist you to get through the maze of requirements and paperwork. That investment should pay off well for you. Oh and one more thing, as you can summarize by now government business is expensive to produce for the agents. MY practice is to pay the agents and bureaus MORE because of this. They deserve it. Time is money!

CHAPTER 24

Travel Tips for The Road Warrior

As much as I love leisure travel, I rarely enjoy business travel like I did when I was much younger because I was naïve, blissful, and ignorant. Now I am mature and aware that we don't live in safe or simple times. The world is a more dangerous place, so I pay attention to travel alerts, make sure I have all the correct and updated travel documents with back-ups in secure places, and much more.

Here are some good tips:

Make two photocopies of all your travel documents in case of emergency or if your documents are lost or stolen. Leave one copy with a friend or relative at home, and make sure they have a working fax machine.

Anytime I travel abroad or in the USA, I have a special travel pack with copies of everything, extra credit cards, and cash in a FedEx envelope that is ready to be sent to me if I need it. You just never know.

It is always a great idea to let at least one person know exactly where you will be staying and how to contact you in an emergency. Carry the other copy with you stored separately from the originals. Documents to make copies of include:

- ☐ Passport ID page

- ☐ Foreign visa (if applicable)

- ☐ Itinerary

- ☐ Hotel confirmation

- ☐ Airline ticket

- ☐ Driver's license

- ☐ Credit cards brought on the trip

- ☐ Travelers check serial numbers

Have a back-up set of critical documents with a trusted family member or assistant.

Always be prepared for emergencies. I usually hire qualified and secure drivers in foreign lands. In certain places I have traveled with security and even bodyguards.

Make sure you have the contact information for the nearest U.S. Embassy or Consulate where you are going. Consular duty personnel are available for emergency assistance 24 hours a day, 7 days a week, at U.S. embassies, consulates, and consular agencies overseas and in Washington, D.C. Contact information for U.S. embassies, consulates, and consular agencies overseas may be found in our Country Specific Information pages.

If your family needs to reach you because of an emergency at home or if they are worried about your welfare, they should call the Office of Overseas Citizens Services in Washington, D.C. at 1-888-407-4747 (during business hours) or 202-647-5225 (after hours).

The State Department will relay the message to the consular officers in the country where you are.

The consular officers will then try to locate you, pass on any urgent messages, and, if you wish, report back to your family in accordance with the Privacy Act.

Vaccinations Are Required for Entry to Some Countries.

Some countries require foreign visitors to carry an International Certificate of Vaccination (aka Yellow Card) or other proof that they have had certain inoculations or medical tests before entering or transiting their country.

Before you travel, check the Country Specific Information and contact the foreign embassy of the country to be visited or transited through for current entry requirements.

Health experts recommend vaccinations for travel to some countries.

The U.S. Centers for Disease Control (CDC) and the World Health Organization (WHO) can provide you their recommendations for vaccinations and other travel health precautions for your trip abroad.

Are you taking any prescription or other medications?

If you take prescription medication:

Pack enough to last your entire trip, including some extra in case you are unexpectedly delayed.

Carry your medications in their original labeled containers, and pack them in your carry-on bag since checked baggage is occasionally lost or delayed.

Ask your pharmacy or physician for the generic equivalent name of your prescriptions in case you need to purchase additional medication abroad.

Get a letter from your physician in case you are questioned about your carry-on medication; some countries have strict restrictions on bringing prescription or even non-prescription medications into the country without proper medical documentation.

Pack smart and pack light so you can move quickly and have a free hand when you need it.

Carry a minimum number of valuables and plan places to conceal them. Money belts work well for this.

Use covered luggage tags to avoid casual observation of your identity and nationality.

Avoid packing IDs, tickets, and other vital documents in backpacks or other locations you won't be able to see at all times. I keep documents in a chest pocket with a button or velcro, and on occasion use a lanyard-like badge holder around my neck, that I can tuck into my shirt.

Pick an airline points program and stick to it. The more you travel using the same airline, the more benefits you'll derive from the points program — like upgrades, early boarding and other perks that can make travel less stressful.

It might be wise to focus on the airline that has the most destinations from your home base.

Balance being realistic and practical with frugal. If you're staying overnight, it may seem smart to choose the cheapest hotel room, but if the hotel is an hour-long cab ride from your meetings, it may not be worth it. Same with the inexpensive flight, it may not be worth it if it takes you twice as long to get where you're going.

In summary: Travel is about style, strategy, philosophy, cooperation, collaboration, travel rewards programs, using good weather apps, and common sense decisions.

A lot of it is simply remembering the Boy Scouts time-honored motto: Be prepared.

CHAPTER 25

Who Wants to be a Multi-Millionaire?
The Tom Antion Effect!

More than 20 years ago I attended a seminar Tom produced and promoted called the "Butt Camp" Seminar with Tom Antion.

That's not a typo. He called it "Butt Camp" because he teaches you how to sit on your butt and make money.

Tom was one of the best teachers, trainers, and experts in the world of public speaking. I have been grateful for over 20 years to call Tom a trusted advisor.

If you ever have the opportunity to attend one of his seminars, boot camps or butt camps, I believe you would find it a good use of your time and resources.

Over the years, Tom has risen to the top of the industry as one of the most respected marketing experts and Internet entrepreneurs.

It is safe to say Tom has semi-retired and is not speaking much these days. He doesn't have to. Because of his enormous back of the room sales when he does speak, he continues to be in the top ranks of high paid speakers.

He demonstrated his willingness to do more and to be a better partner with speakers' bureaus than most other speakers. Tom was the first speaker who delivered to us a separate and uniquely branded video for each topic he spoke on.

Tom has been and continues to be a leader in the speaking industry and a leader in how to produce multiple streams of income.

Over the years, I have participated in his seminars and workshops. I have watched his webinars and read his books. I have bought his programs and training materials. Each time he delivered good value for my investment.

Dollar for dollar and pound for pound, Tom Antion is one of the best in the industry.

You can find Tom at Antion.com, and I suggest you sign up for his mailing list.

Summary: When Tom speaks, we listen. In Tom Antion We Trust.

CHAPTER 26

Someone to Watch Over Me -
The Secret to Faster Success
How to select, build, and maintain
an Advisory Board.

First question is, DO YOU NEED AN ADVISORY BOARD?

The answer is: no, you don't need one.

But you should want one!

Allow me to provide you with a few key reasons to start, build, and maintain an advisory board.

1. They will assist you to see what you don't see.
2. They will support you and assist you to make things happen.
3. They will introduce you to people you need or want to know.
4. They will invite you places you would love to go.
5. They can assist you to establish credibility faster.

6. In the process, you will make some long-term, lifelong friends.
7. They will hold you accountable.

And there is more.

So how do you choose them?

How do you connect and work with them?

How do you organize it?

The best advice I can give you is choose people who have accomplished what you want to do so they can guide you, help you see better ways, and avoid the pitfalls of life and business. Choose people who are strong where you need assistance. Choose people with experience.

Make sure the board understands their role: general oversight and policy formation, not management.

Make sure they understand they have no fiduciary responsibility, and they have no power to vote. They are there to advise you on important business matters.

Each person should be hand-picked by you for maximum diversity of philosophy, geography, expertise, race, and sex.

There is one addition to this: Choose people who have accomplished something big. It is also important to me that they have also overcome a difficult time in their lives. The death of a loved one, a difficult divorce, a tough bankruptcy, a prisoner of war, a recovered alcoholic, or a failed business represent examples of a tough time. These are the people who know what it is like to be down, but not out.

They used free will to rise like a phoenix from the ashes, to climb the ladder of success, and overcome life's adversity. These are people with true character, who can assist you on your journey and through your tough times.

Next, you want people who will challenge you. And you must have the guts to give them permission to tell you the truth, to prevent you from getting hurt and prevent you from making mistakes. And you must be willing to listen to them.

My first advisory board many years ago included the Chairman and President of a Fortune 100 company, an old and wise football coach, a street-smart minister who was a psychologist and counselor, a former athlete and health food expert who had gone into personal training, and a dentist who has strong business experience, but also had good experience with nonprofit groups and the education marketplace. Plus, this dentist was the president of the Montessori Board and he assisted me on many levels. And finally, I asked a woman of Asian descent with a very diverse business background and an African American Professor of Media to join the board.

Each person brought uniqueness to the table that I did not have and needed assistance with.

Over time, I had some other great people on the board. We invited several great speakers, a couple of great agents, and a few speakers' bureau owners who were in the twilight of their career. They were very giving and supportive with great advice and wisdom.

Along the way, I had techie gurus. Most were terrific on the many challenges we faced.

As I reflect on doing this for many years, one of the best advisory board members was the football coach. While his time was very limited, especially during football season, Coach was extremely supportive of my efforts and taught me efficient ways to work with the rest of the board.

I watched him coach the players and manage the assistant coaches. I watched him work with the school administration, the alumni, parents, teachers, law enforcement, and with the media. He had all these people's expectations to manage; plus, Coach was very instrumental in assisting me to see the big picture and run the company.

After working with him for a year, Coach invited me to join him for the last week of pre-season practice. He asked me to deliver the locker-room speech before the first game of the season.

I should note here: the team won the season opener and shut-out their opponent 35 to nothing. While I still believe it was a great speech that inspired the team, it was a great team effort. I never touched the ball on the field. In the locker room after the game, they gave me a game ball. So, in some small way, I was able to pay back the coach for what he shared with me. The team had a great season, and I was proud to be a part of it.

That gets me to a very important point. Be willing to give back, look for ways to give back, and do more for them than they are doing for you. Remember, don't bite the hand that feeds you, kiss it instead."

"For it is in giving that we receive." Francis of Assisi

Next tip: Put time limits on the term. One and two year limits have worked out well. I start out by asking for one year. You will be able to tell how it is working within three to six months. If it is going well, at nine months you can ask for an extension. If not then you only have three more months to go.

I always made the effort to stay in touch with them after their term ended. More than half of them became life-long friends.

In one case, a board member who had been with us for less than a year had to move away and quit her job in order to look after her ailing older brother. He was not expected to make it, but according to the accounts, he had a miraculous recovery. She told us the things that helped her keep going was what she learned from us and hoped we would invite her back soon. It was one of those times that galvanized the group.

"Talent wins games, but teamwork and intelligence wins championships."
Michael Jordon

Next, while you are working with your current board members, you should be on the constant look out for future advisors. Keeping the pipeline full should be a top priority for you.

Don't be shy about asking them to introduce you to the right people and business opportunities. Be sure you do the same thing for them. Remember, don't bite the hand that feeds you, kiss it instead.

In 1999, I had an awakening as I answered the phone at the Bureau on a Friday afternoon. It was about 3 o'clock, and I was looking forward to the end of the day after a very challenging week. As I was reflecting on this ball-buster of a week, all the phone lines are lit up. I answered line three. The person on the other end (I could tell by the voice it was a young female) said in a sharp voice, "We need to book a speaker, what do you got?"

I was taken aback by her lack of civility for a moment, and then I said, "Well we have Zig Ziglar; he's $65,000. How does that sound?"

And she said, "Never heard of him."

I was speechless. Well, I gasped and said, "One moment please, I'll connect you with someone that can assist you."

After putting her on hold, I reached into my left desk drawer and pulled out an oxygen mask and started sucking on it hard. In this moment of blazing clarity, I realized that Gen X is now active in the marketplace. I need to figure out how to connect with these young people.

In hindsight, I could have said Snoop Dogg or Madonna, and they might have said, "Oh wow, they do motivational speaking?" But I wasn't that quick at that moment. I have to admit I was shell-shocked, I thought everybody knew Zig.

However, what I ended up saying was, "Vicky, pick up line number three, I'm taking the dog for a walk." So, I let Vicky work the call.

At the time, I had an old golden retriever named Bubba.

You know how sometimes you talk to your dog when you're going for a walk? It's just you and your dog. They look up at you like they understand you? At that moment, Bubba seemed empathetic; in Bubba's case, he was an old, wise soul. He probably thought I was nuts for just ranting and rambling on and on.

As we walked for a long time, I silently processed this phone conversation, playing it over and over and over again in my mind. Finally, I looked down at Bubba the old dog, and I said, "Well Bubba, I guess it's official, I'm an old dog."

Old Bubba looked up at me and said, "You just figure that out? Really, you're just figuring that out now?"

Well, upon my return from the insightful walk with Bubba, I called a couple board members, and we made plans for dinner.

We talked about the week, the month, and what was going on in our lives and businesses. After dinner, we had a nice walk in the park. I brought up the topic of what happened that day, and asked if they could advise me on how to proceed and what they might recommend.

They didn't have much for me at the moment. Then it hit me, I'm sitting here asking my advisors for assistance. In another moment of blazing clarity (two in one day is so rare!), I realized I must establish a GEN X Advisory Board.

I need a whole new extra board. A new group of young people who are getting into business and have enough experience they can assist me in understanding their values, what's important to them, how they think about the world, and how they look at things. I became very excited.

I set out on the path. I contacted my current advisers with a memo about the plan. Each one of them thought it was a great idea. Some offered suggestions and recommendations.

A few of them offered to give me their kids, "for as long as you want them," their memo stated.

Within six months, I had eight Gen X advisory board members. Now, I must admit it was a very different experience. They were good; they were sharp, and they were young. They didn't have the benefit of many experiences compared to the other board, but they had just what I wanted and needed. Plus, they had energy, stamina, fresh ideas, and a 'why not try it out curiosity' that exceeded my expectations.

So there you have it. The advisory board is one of my best strategies to becoming a better professional, making more money, building your network of trusted advisors, and minimizing your mistakes.

In summary: Commit to doing it. Choose the best people you can. Be willing to cut your losses if it is not working out. Don't burn your bridges. Look for ways to give back to them. Give them more than they are giving to you.

I wish you well.

P.S. This is your opportunity to build and create the life you want and the time to start is now.

CHAPTER 27

The Ending of All Endings
Achieving your potential: You need a plan!

The greatest waste of our resources is the number of people or companies that never achieve their potential.

Not only never achieve it, but also don't even put forth the effort.

Someone has a great idea, and someone else says it can't be done. Gather enough reasons why it can't be done, and sure enough it won't be done, won't even be attempted.

In the 1960's John F. Kennedy challenged the country and scientific community with, "Let's put a man on the moon in this decade."

The immediate consequence was predictable, "Can't be done, it's unrealistic, not enough time, to many unanswered questions."

One statistician estimated that over 50 million separate decisions, operations, and activities, would have to be coordinated in order to design, produce, launch and safely land a planetary expedition.

That's a pretty good reason not to try. But they tried anyway. They had a plan. Lots and lots of plans! High intentions set the universe in motion; I'm not talking about God or a higher power. I'm talking about you and me. What we dream about and what we act on. I'm talking about you and me, about all the ordinary everyday people who pursue or fail to pursue their biggest dreams or brightest aspirations.

Kennedy's lunar aspiration was so big and so exciting that it galvanized the worldwide scientific community, setting the necessary wheels in motion to achieve it.

How exciting are your dreams? Exciting enough to override all the reasons and excuses? We can assist each other and set the wheels in motion. We can say: "It will never fly," or "We will never know until we try."

We can say: "It's never been done before." Or we can take the opportunity to be the first.

We can say: "I don't have the resources." Or "Let's be resourceful."

We can say "I don't have the expertise." Or we can network with those who do.

We only pass this way once. If you believe in something good, then give it a chance to happen. When you look back on your life, you'll regret the things you didn't do more than the ones you did.

Thank you for reading this book. I truly hope you found it valuable.

Please get in touch with our organization, if you believe we might assist you in the future.

www.speakersbureau.com

www.publicspeakingformoney.com

www.frankcandy.com

Also, I invite you to connect with me in Social Media

The Most Incredible Gift Ever – a $297.00 VALUE You may choose any ONE of the following:

1. A 20-minute call with one of the marketing experts on our team to discuss your brand and positioning statement, or marketing kit, or the possibility for representation in the future. It would be good if you had the clear answers to the list of questions at the end of Chapter 4.
2. A review and evaluation of your demo video by our marketing experts. Note: the video length must not be more than 6 minutes long. You may accomplish this by sending an email of a link to your demo video, along with your media kit to us.
3. A **ONE-TIME ONLY** $297.00 discount on one of our consulting packages. See the web site.

www.publicspeakingformoney.com/gift

The email address is: info@publicspeakingformoney.com

We look forward to hearing from you.

Frank Candy

www.speakersbureau.com

www.publicspeakingformoney.com

www.frankcandy.com

Also, I invite you to connect with me in Social Media